# WHAT OTHERS ARE SAYING

I've watched Vince Hudson apply world-class brand strategy for decades on some of the world's best brands. In *Date Like a Brand*, he brings that same purpose and passion to relationships—with powerful, provocative insights that only he could deliver.

—Jim Stengel,
President/CEO
The Jim Stengel Company
(former CMO of Procter and Gamble)

I was lucky enough to know Vince—and get the blueprint for this framework—long before it became a book. I was at a life stage where I needed to relaunch my dating brand with intention. Using these principles, I found clarity, showed up with purpose, and built a relationship that blossomed into a beautiful marriage and family. This isn't theory—it's a framework that works.

—Gail Frasier Cox
Marketing Executive

Vince Hudson doesn't just shift the dating conversation—he rebrands it. *Date Like a Brand* offers the kind of strategic frameworks we use to launch cultural movements, now applied to love. I'm living these principles, and they're a game-changer. If you want to approach relationships with the same intentionality that drives brand success, this is your new playbook.

—Alisa Jacobs
Co-Founder & Co-CEO, Loop
Culture Strategist & Brand Architect

# DATE LIKE A BRAND

*A Powerful Marketing Framework for Finding and Keeping the Love of Your Life*

# DATE LIKE A BRAND

*A Powerful Marketing Framework for Finding and Keeping the Love of Your Life*

**VINCE HUDSON**

ethos
collective

DATE LIKE A BRAND © 2025 by Vince Hudson. All rights reserved.

Printed in the United States of America

Published by Igniting Souls
PO Box 43, Powell, OH 43065
IgnitingSouls.com

This book contains material protected under international and federal copyright laws and treaties. Any unauthorized reprint or use of this material is prohibited. No part of this book may be reproduced or transmitted in any form or by any means, electronic or mechanical, including photocopying, recording, or by any information storage and retrieval system, without express written permission from the author.

LCCN: 2025905097
Paperback ISBN: 978-1-63680-483-5
Hardback ISBN: 978-1-63680-484-2
eBook ISBN: 978-1-63680-485-9

Available in paperback, hardcover, e-book, and audiobook.

Any Internet addresses (websites, blogs, etc.) and telephone numbers printed in this book are offered as a resource. They are not intended in any way to be or imply an endorsement by Igniting Souls, nor does Igniting Souls vouch for the content of these sites and numbers for the life of this book.

Some names and identifying details may have been changed to protect the privacy of individuals.

The superscript symbol IP listed throughout this book is known as the unique certification mark created and owned by Instant IP™. Its use signifies that the corresponding expression (words, phrases, chart, graph, etc.) has been protected by Instant IP™ via smart contract. Instant IP™ is designed with the patented smart contract solution (US Patent: 11,928,748), which creates an immutable time-stamped first layer and fast layer identifying the moment in time an idea is filed on the blockchain. This solution can be used in defending intellectual property protection. Infringing upon the respective intellectual property, i.e., IP, is subject to and punishable in a court of law.

Because your BRAND is so deserving of GREAT LOVE,
this book was given to you by

_____

*This book is dedicated to my amazing daughters:
Olivia, Ava, and Vanna.*

I know I told you this book is about "dating,"
but as you know, dating is a "no-no" for a long time.
The book is really about "growing."

As you grow towards love, it will grow towards you.

God's gift of daughters, so wise and true
I pen these pages as a gift for you.
The world of love is vast and wide
with twists and turns, where hearts collide.

As you grow and one day date,
may these lessons illuminate.
I pray the scene will start to change
with kindness growing in love's reign.

My sweet girls, you deserve the best,
a love that stands life's trying tests.
For love, like brands, must hold its ground
in purpose clear and truth profound.

When you don't know what to do,
love's first rule says first love you!
True love will arrive strong and true.
It will bring out the best in you.

I have one hope, one wish, one plea,
that each of you will grow to be
confident women filled with love
with a life fulfilled from up above.

# CONTENTS

Foreword by Dr. Brenda Wade . . . . . . . . . . . . . . . . . . . . . xvii
A Note to the Reader . . . . . . . . . . . . . . . . . . . . . . . . . . . . . .xxi
    Love as a Movement . . . . . . . . . . . . . . . . . . . . . . . xxiii

## PART ONE: MARKET UNDERSTANDING

Chapter One: Dating Isn't Easy. . . . . . . . . . . . . . . . . . . 3
    Technology Hasn't Made Relationships Easier. . . . . 5
    Love Will Not Find a Way, You Need a Strategy . . . 6
    Defining Love . . . . . . . . . . . . . . . . . . . . . . . . . . . . 8
    Reframe Our Thinking . . . . . . . . . . . . . . . . . . . . 11
    Take Action. . . . . . . . . . . . . . . . . . . . . . . . . . . . . 13
Chapter Two: Understanding the Paradigm Shift . . . . . 15
    The Crowded Shelf . . . . . . . . . . . . . . . . . . . . . . . 16
    You Don't Have to Sell Yourself. . . . . . . . . . . . . . 18
    You Are a Brand . . . . . . . . . . . . . . . . . . . . . . . . 20
    Take Action. . . . . . . . . . . . . . . . . . . . . . . . . . . . . 23

## PART TWO: BRAND PLANNING

Chapter Three: Pre-Assessment, Part One. . . . . . . . . . . 27
    The Deep Dive Into the Category . . . . . . . . . . . . 29
    The Deep Dive Into the Consumer . . . . . . . . . . . 31
    What This Means for Dating Consumers
       in the 21st Century . . . . . . . . . . . . . . . . . . . . . 33

    Marketing to the Access Generation . . . . . . . . . . . 35
    Assessing the VUCA of the Dating Scene . . . . . . . 37
    Take Action. . . . . . . . . . . . . . . . . . . . . . . . . . . . . . 39

Chapter Four: Pre-Assessment Part Two . . . . . . . . . . . 41
    The Fruits Are in the Roots:
        Your Brand Foundation. . . . . . . . . . . . . . . . . . 42
    The Relationship Imprint . . . . . . . . . . . . . . . . . . 43
    Imprints Influence Your Attachment Style. . . . . . . 44
    Understanding Attachment Styles . . . . . . . . . . . . . 45
    The Secure Attachment Style . . . . . . . . . . . . . . . . 46
    The Anxious Attachment Style . . . . . . . . . . . . . . . 48
    The Avoidant Attachment Style . . . . . . . . . . . . . . 49
    The Disorganized Attachment Style . . . . . . . . . . . 50
    Making Your Attachment Style a Strength. . . . . . . 51
    Your Attachment Style Is Not Set in Stone . . . . . . 54
    Take Action. . . . . . . . . . . . . . . . . . . . . . . . . . . . . . 55

Chapter Five: Purpose. . . . . . . . . . . . . . . . . . . . . . . . . . 58
    What Does Success Look Like?. . . . . . . . . . . . . . . 59
    How to Find Love For Your Life . . . . . . . . . . . . . 60
    Growing Together . . . . . . . . . . . . . . . . . . . . . . . . 61
    Take Action. . . . . . . . . . . . . . . . . . . . . . . . . . . . . . 63

Chapter Six: Positioning . . . . . . . . . . . . . . . . . . . . . . . 64
    Your Personal USP. . . . . . . . . . . . . . . . . . . . . . . . 65
    The Dating Value Proposition . . . . . . . . . . . . . . . 66
    The Dating Value Proposition Compass. . . . . . . . . 70
    Understanding the Bell Curve . . . . . . . . . . . . . . . 73
    Take Action. . . . . . . . . . . . . . . . . . . . . . . . . . . . . . 78

Chapter Seven: Assessing the Mind. . . . . . . . . . . . . . . 80
    Understanding the Two Components of the Mind. . 81
    Expanding Your Mental Value . . . . . . . . . . . . . . . 86
    Take Action. . . . . . . . . . . . . . . . . . . . . . . . . . . . . . 88

Chapter Eight: Assessing the Body ............... 90
   The Two Main Ways to Assess the Body ........ 90
   The Body Bell Curve ...................... 91
   The Difficult Truth ....................... 98
   Improving Your Body Value ................ 101
   Take Action ............................ 102

Chapter Nine: Assessing Your Resources ........... 104
   The Two Tiers of Resources ................ 105
   The Reality Check of the Resources Bell Curve .. 106
   Assessing Your Current Resources ........... 110
   Increase Your Resources Score .............. 112
   Take Action ............................ 113

Chapter Ten: Assessing the Soul ................. 115
   The Dimensions of the Soul ............... 116
   The Soul Score: Ten Levels of Internal Maturity .. 120
   Why Soul Matters in a Relationship ......... 124
   Strengthening Your Soul Component ........ 125
   Take Action ............................ 128

Chapter Eleven: Measuring the Strength
of the Relationship ........................ 131
   Measure the Relationship ................. 132
   The Passion Scale ....................... 134
   The Decision Scale ...................... 136
   The Friendship Scale ..................... 137
   The Scorecard .......................... 138
   What It Means ......................... 139
   Take Action ............................ 139

Chapter Twelve: The Dating Value
Proposition Lifecycle ....................... 140
   Gender Plays a Role ..................... 141
   The Five Stages of the DVP Lifecycle ........ 143

    Playing to Your Life Stage . . . . . . . . . . . . . . . . . . 150
    Understanding the Two Crisis Cycles
        of the Lifecycle . . . . . . . . . . . . . . . . . . . . . . . . 150
    The Dating Zone Matrix . . . . . . . . . . . . . . . . . . . 153
    Take Action . . . . . . . . . . . . . . . . . . . . . . . . . . . . 154

Chapter Thirteen: Let's Play: The DVP Market
Chips Game . . . . . . . . . . . . . . . . . . . . . . . . . . . . . . . . 157
    I Need More than Twenty Chips! . . . . . . . . . . . . 159
    Your Perceived Market Worth . . . . . . . . . . . . . . 160
    Take Action . . . . . . . . . . . . . . . . . . . . . . . . . . . . 160

Chapter Fourteen: Performance Dating . . . . . . . . . . . 162
    Performance Standards . . . . . . . . . . . . . . . . . . . 163
    Don't Use Vanity Metrics . . . . . . . . . . . . . . . . . . 165
    Take Action . . . . . . . . . . . . . . . . . . . . . . . . . . . . 166

Chapter Fifteen: Factors That Impact
Performance Dating . . . . . . . . . . . . . . . . . . . . . . . . . . 168
    The Role of Sampling . . . . . . . . . . . . . . . . . . . . 168
    Time and Testing . . . . . . . . . . . . . . . . . . . . . . . . 172
    Factoring in the Two Systems of Marketing . . . . . 174
    The Role of "Consultants" in Dating . . . . . . . . . . 178
    Take Action . . . . . . . . . . . . . . . . . . . . . . . . . . . . 181

Chapter Sixteen: The Four Agreements
of Dating Like a Brand . . . . . . . . . . . . . . . . . . . . . . . 183
    Agreement 1: Be Impeccable with Your Word . . . 184
    Agreement 2: Don't Take Anything Personally . . . 185
    Agreement 3: Don't Make Assumptions . . . . . . . . 186
    Agreement 4: Always Do Your Best . . . . . . . . . . . 187
    Take Action . . . . . . . . . . . . . . . . . . . . . . . . . . . . 189

## PART THREE: GO TO MARKET

Chapter Seventeen: The Six Launch Gates
of True Love . . . . . . . . . . . . . . . . . . . . . . . . . . . . . . . 193

   Before the Gates: Get Market-Ready. . . . . . . . . . 194
   Gate One: Discovery—Swipe Left and
      Pay Attention to Chance Encounters. . . . . . . . 195
   Gate Two: Validation—Real-Life Dating
      Without Commitment . . . . . . . . . . . . . . . . . . 196
   Gate Three: The Test Market—Exclusive Dating,
      Strategic Evaluation . . . . . . . . . . . . . . . . . . . . 197
   Gate Four: Engagement—Launch Agreement
      and Execution Mode. . . . . . . . . . . . . . . . . . . 199
   Gate Five: Wedding: The Launch and
      Celebration of a Public Partnership. . . . . . . . . 201
   Gate Six: Co-Partnering for Growth—
      The Strategy for Long-Term Marriage . . . . . . 201
   Action Steps . . . . . . . . . . . . . . . . . . . . . . . . . . . . 204

Chapter Eighteen: Partnership Marketing
in Marriage. . . . . . . . . . . . . . . . . . . . . . . . . . . . . . . 205

   Not a Big Bang . . . . . . . . . . . . . . . . . . . . . . . . . 206
   Love Is a Language . . . . . . . . . . . . . . . . . . . . . . 206
   More Partnership Strategies. . . . . . . . . . . . . . . . 208
   Micro-Moments That Build Macro Love. . . . . . . 209
   Action Steps . . . . . . . . . . . . . . . . . . . . . . . . . . . . 212

Chapter Nineteen: The Annual Relationship Review. . 213

   Part I: Reassessing Your Dating
      Value Proposition . . . . . . . . . . . . . . . . . . . . . 214
   Part II: Taking the Temperature of the
      Relationship by Evaluating the Passion,
      Friendship, and Decision. . . . . . . . . . . . . . . . 215
   Set Annual Goals—Together or Solo. . . . . . . . . . 215
   Take Action. . . . . . . . . . . . . . . . . . . . . . . . . . . . 216

Chapter Twenty: The Circle of Love For Life . . . . . . . 217
   Phase One of the Circle of Love For Life:
      Love of Self. . . . . . . . . . . . . . . . . . . . . . . . . . . 218
   Phase Two of the Circle of Love For Life:
      Love of Source . . . . . . . . . . . . . . . . . . . . . . . 219
   Phase Three in the Circle of Love For Life:
      Love of Mate . . . . . . . . . . . . . . . . . . . . . . . . 220
   Phase Four of the Circle of Love For Life:
      Love of Legacy . . . . . . . . . . . . . . . . . . . . . . . 221
   Circle of Love For Life—Target, Objective,
      and Output . . . . . . . . . . . . . . . . . . . . . . . . . . 223
   Take Action. . . . . . . . . . . . . . . . . . . . . . . . . . . . 224

BONUS CHAPTER:
How It All Began—"The Vinnifer Story" . . . . . . . . . . 227
   Discovering My Own DVP and PDF . . . . . . . . . 228
   Discovery: One Night in New Orleans . . . . . . . . 229
   The Validation Period . . . . . . . . . . . . . . . . . . . . 230
   The Breakup . . . . . . . . . . . . . . . . . . . . . . . . . . 231
   Separate Paths, Parallel Growth. . . . . . . . . . . . . 231
   Test Market 2.0—The Comeback . . . . . . . . . . . 232
   Enter Pre-Launch and Launch . . . . . . . . . . . . . 232
   Loyalty: Building Real Life Together. . . . . . . . . . 233
   Write Your Own Story. . . . . . . . . . . . . . . . . . . . 233
   A Change, A Movement—Learn More . . . . . . . . 234

Acknowledgments . . . . . . . . . . . . . . . . . . . . . . . . . 237
Endnotes. . . . . . . . . . . . . . . . . . . . . . . . . . . . . . . . 239
About the Author . . . . . . . . . . . . . . . . . . . . . . . . . 243

# FOREWORD BY DR. BRENDA WADE

When I first met Vince and Jennifer back in 2008, they were dating—again. They had just weathered a long breakup but clearly still had deep feelings for one another. It was beautiful to witness their love renewal after the ups and downs. I had no idea then how intertwined our lives would become.

We met during a fashion and beauty-themed event where I was a featured speaker. Vince's company sponsored the event, and he was introduced to me as the Marketing Director of COVERGIRL. Naturally, I was intrigued—how often do you meet a man running a cosmetics brand who is genuinely passionate about both beauty and relationships? I couldn't wait to meet him.

When we finally connected, it was instant. Vince had an energy—a rare blend of heart and strategy. His love for marketing wasn't just about selling products; it was about understanding people, emotion, perception, and connection. The fact that he led a beauty brand made it all the more fitting, but what stood out most was his curiosity about how all this fit into human love relationships.

For over two decades, I've been a psychologist, TV host, and guest expert for many national programs and have written and co-authored multiple books on love. These years dedicated to helping people heal and grow their intimate connection are joyful. So, when Vince shared that he had a dream to write a dating book, I'll admit—I was a little skeptical. After all, he wasn't a psychologist, and he was still single. But the more we talked, the more I realized: this wasn't just a marketer dabbling in dating advice. Vince saw patterns. He saw the emotions and thinking patterns behind attraction, loyalty, and decision-making in ways most people overlook. This was exciting!

We began comparing notes—my lens as a psychologist and his as a brand strategist. The parallels between marketing and dating were undeniable. Over time, we even presented together at an MBA conference, our ideas weaving together in a yin-yang balance of clinical insight and creative strategy. I encouraged him then to write this book, but he had some life to live first.

The day came when he told me he was going to propose to Jennifer. And yes, he was super nervous!

From the beginning, I knew Jennifer was extraordinary—brilliant, graceful, grounded, and radiant from the inside out. What I didn't know then was that I would get to walk alongside them in their marriage, witness the birth of their three beautiful daughters, and even serve as their counselor during the highs and lows that every real relationship faces. I can't share the private moments, of course, but I can say this: Vince and Jennifer have lived the very framework this book teaches. They've applied it, tested it, and grown from it.

In fact, I was the one who encouraged Vince to include their love story in these pages. I knew it would mirror that of so many—it isn't perfect, but it's real. He had to practice what he preaches, and that authenticity gives this book a beating heart. It's one thing to teach a framework—it's another to embody it in your own life. And Vince did just that.

That's what makes *Date Like a Brand* so powerful. It's not just a theory. It's a lived philosophy.

Vince hasn't reinvented relationship science—he's woven together what works, built on timeless principles, and layered in marketing wisdom that makes it fresh, intuitive, and best

## Foreword by Dr. Brenda Wade

of all, remarkably actionable. Whether you're just starting to date, healing from heartbreak, trying to figure out why your "type" keeps missing the mark, or hitting refresh on your love relationship, this book is your mirror and your map.

Love is an evolutionary journey. You will grow and evolve more as a person, and your love will keep growing and evolving if you commit to being a "lifelong love learner." Having witnessed Vince's journey unfold over nearly two decades, I'm delighted that you get to have this book in your hands. You get to learn more about relationships and love from one of the most thoughtful, intentional, and creative minds I've had the privilege to know. I'm so proud to stand beside Vince and this important love message.

—Dr. Brenda Wade
Media Host and Guest, Author, Relationship Expert, and Founder of Love & Relationship Global Training Programs

# A NOTE TO THE READER

In March 2005, Greg Behrendt, author of *He's Just Not That Into You,* appeared on *The Oprah Winfrey Show.* My friend Candi, one of the producers, knew I had read the book, and not only was I "aggressively single," I also had the equivalent of a PhD in relationship literature. She asked me to be on the show to discuss the book's impact on my dating life. Three days later, I found myself sitting with ten female panelists, Mr. Behrendt, and Oprah Winfrey herself.

Greg captivated the audience by explaining how men's lame excuses often boil down to one simple truth: they're "just not that into you." The panelist closest to me, a superfan of the book, turned and said, "Wow! This is super-helpful." I curiously asked, "What made it really helpful?" She replied, "Now I know that NONE of the guys I liked were really into me."

I said, "Great, now that you know, what do you do next?" Silence. She sat perplexed, then finally admitted, "I really don't know."

That's when it hit me. We need a bolder objective. It's not enough to just figure out who isn't into you. You have to find the one person who is. Greg's book provides Step One: the reality check. But what's Step Two?

I had been studying relationships for years, and I knew I had to use what I'd learned to answer that question. I considered calling the book *He's Just Not That Into You . . . Now*

*What?* But I wasn't a relationship expert, a comedian, or a psychologist. So, I just let it go.

At first.

Shortly after my Winfrey appearance, I read a business article entitled "Is Loyalty Dead?" It explored the erosion of consumer loyalty due to overwhelming options, fierce competition, and ever-changing expectations. The insights hit me hard; I realized relationships faced the same dynamics.

In my journey as a marketer, I came across a brilliant idea brought to life in Kevin Roberts's book *Lovemarks*. Roberts, a businessman at the helm of Saatchi & Saatchi, redefined the world of marketing by arguing that the most successful brands weren't just trusted—they were loved. He introduced the concept that brands needed to move beyond logic and reason to create emotional bonds with consumers.

His theory captivated me. This businessman boldly talked about love as the key to success in business, suggesting we turn abstract feelings into actionable strategies. And I wondered: if love could make us better marketers, then perhaps marketing could make us better lovers, or, I should say, better at finding love.

I feel fortunate to have met Kevin Roberts years ago. When I told him about my idea to reverse his approach using marketing concepts to help people become better lovers and partners, he chuckled. Today, he might not remember our conversation, but I've carried the inspiration ever since. *Lovemarks* challenged me to think deeply about connections, loyalty, and relationships, and it planted the seed for this book.

At one time or another, we've all been blocked by one simple line in a job posting: "Previous Experience Required." Let's face it—no one wants to hire someone who is just theorizing about the work without having actually done it. I had the same problem when this idea formed twenty years ago.

# A Note to the Reader

I knew I was hardly qualified to share my ideas. Who wants to take relationship advice from someone who's still swiping and figuring things out?

So, I did what any good researcher would do—I put the principles to use. I dated (a lot), I got married (once), had daughters (three of them), and invested years (over fifteen) in field-testing my theories. After spending so much time in the trenches of relationships, my theories have become battle-tested strategies that prove the connection between building a lasting relationship and brand loyalty. The only real difference is you can't hold a "buy-one-get-one" to boost sales when things get rocky in marriage.

Great brands have found ways to achieve consumer loyalty. And *Date Like a Brand* captures those techniques to transform the search for love from a game of chance into a strategic pursuit. Whether you're single, newly divorced, or in a relationship looking to level up, this clear, actionable framework will help you find and keep the right partner, allowing you to launch a relationship that lasts way past the wedding day.

The best relationships aren't achieved by luck—they're discovered and built through strategy, intention, and understanding. Great brands develop lasting connections with their audience, and I want to help you create an even richer, more meaningful lasting connection with your ideal partner. To that end, I suggest you and I start a movement.

## Love as a Movement

Because here's the thing: This isn't just about you. When you approach love strategically to find the right person, build a strong partnership, and invest in the relationship, you're not just improving your own life. You're contributing to something much bigger.

Strong relationships lead to strong families.

Strong families create supportive communities.

And supportive communities? Well, they can change the world. And I mean the whole world. This book is written to be inclusive of people of every nation, culture, and gender identity.

And world-changing ideas need a movement.

I need you to help me spread this message that has the power to move people from the chaos of swiping and shallow connections to clarity, purpose, and lasting relationships. When we Date Like a Brand$^{IP}$, we can replace confusion with confidence, clutter with clear choices, and complexity with criteria-based collaborations.

I have a promise for you: if you take what you're about to read and put it into action, you'll not only have a better understanding of yourself and what you're looking for—you'll also have the tools to build a relationship that lasts.

By the time you finish this book, you'll have:

- A clear framework for evaluating potential partners
- Strategies for assessing and presenting your authentic self effectively
- Tools for building and maintaining a thriving relationship
- Confidence in your dating decisions

Because at the end of the day, love is the greatest brand you'll ever build. And when you get it right, it's not just life-changing—it's world-changing.

# PART ONE

## MARKET UNDERSTANDING

# CHAPTER ONE

# Dating Isn't Easy

*You'll be the prince and I'll be the princess,
It's a love story, baby, just say, "Yes"*
—Taylor Swift's "Love Story"

Growing up, my nickname was "Vince the Prince." The playful rhyme planted a seed in my young mind. Like many of you, my childhood included tales of princes rescuing princesses, overcoming obstacles, and riding off into the sunset together. Every prince had a princess, so my younger self felt confident I would find someone to complete my story.

Unfortunately, fairy tales don't paint an accurate picture of how relationships work. Worse still, they leave out the most critical part—how to ensure you have a happily ever after.

My daughters also love princess stories. Tiana from *The Princess and the Frog* reigned supreme in our house. The hard-working Tiana kisses the frog, meets her prince, and lives happily ever after in the magical world of New Orleans. But every time I watch her story unfold with them, I can't help but feel that, like most fairy tales, the story ends before the real work begins.

I want my girls to understand that true, lasting love lives long beyond riding off on the white steed. [My real love story ironically has New Orleans' fantastical magic, but I'll touch on that later.]

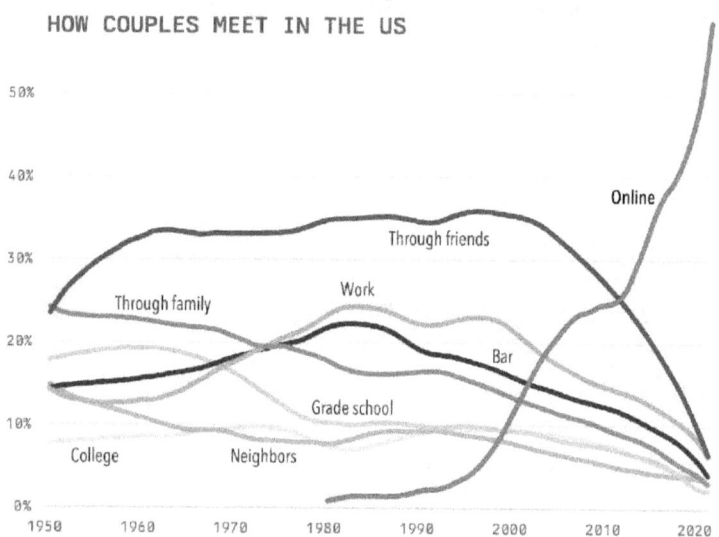

One hundred years ago, couples met at high school or college. Many of our great-grandparents truly married "the girl next door." Church socials and introductions from aunts and uncles topped the list of places to find the love of your life. After women became a strong part of the workforce during World War II, places of employment opened up as spots for couples to meet. Still, even through the 1960s and 1970s, friends and family topped the list of how people met.

## Dating Isn't Easy

During the 1970s, personal ads rose in popularity, but when the technological age surged in the 1990s, the whole dating scene took a major turn. By 2010, nearly 20 percent of couples said they met online, and today, that number is closer to 40 percent.[1]

The history of marketing has a parallel that blows my mind. Back when our ancestors married the boy next door, every little town had a general store. Your choices for products were as limited as your choices for mates. Even car selections got in on the fun. You could have a vehicle in any color you wanted as long as it was a black Model T.

The Industrial Revolution expanded product and dating possibilities. It brought more people into the city, widening the dating pool. The social revolution and women's rights movement of the 1960s forced marketers to begin to look at ladies as part of their target audience and changed the couple dynamic in dating.

In the last few decades, the digital revolution pushed the boundaries of marketing as well as dating, with apps, swiping, and global connection changing everything.

## Technology Hasn't Made Relationships Easier

Technology, shifting gender economics, and cultural expectations have completely reshaped the landscape. Despite technological advancements in the dating world, relationships are not thriving. Divorce rates remain high, and studies indicate people are lonelier than ever. A report from Cigna found that 58 percent of Americans feel lonely, with young adults and single people being the most affected.[2] Even though we're more connected digitally, we've lost much of the emotional depth that sustains long-term relationships.

There are three primary causes of this disjointed connection:

1. **Lack of depth in the relationship:** Texting, swiping, and messaging make initial connections fast and easy, but they often fail to have the nuance that builds trust and emotional intimacy required for lasting relationships.
2. **The relationship becomes superficial:** This lack of face-to-face interaction puts an overemphasis on superficial traits. Just as consumers often choose products based on packaging or ads, daters often prioritize surface-level qualities like appearance or witty bios, overlooking deeper compatibility.
3. **Pressure of the Global Prospect:** While global access to potential partners is exciting, it also creates unrealistic expectations. People feel pressured to find someone perfect when, in reality, relationships are built on shared growth, not perfection. There is NOT a flawless Instagram model waiting for everyone; they are in your phone (and mind), not your actual life.

## Love Will Not Find a Way, You Need a Strategy

We've all heard the saying, "Love will find a way." It's a comforting thought. Everyone would like to think that if love is meant to be, it will somehow overcome all obstacles and, like a self-guided missile, navigate the chaos of modern dating, delivering us straight into the arms of the perfect partner.

The problem with "love will find a way" is that it puts all the responsibility on love and none on us. It's like imagining a hammer will find its way to a nail or an arrow will zero in on a bullseye. But we all know, the only way to hit the target is through skillful aim. It takes action.

## Dating Isn't Easy

Hollywood created an equally bizarre phrase that marketers only hoped would work in the film *Field of Dreams:* "If you build it, they will come." Every entrepreneur wishes they could simply create something that would automatically attract an audience. If that were true, companies wouldn't need to spend billions figuring out how to position their products, reach the right consumers, and build relationships that drive loyalty. And marketers, like me, would be out of a job.

As I mentioned in my note at the beginning, the similarities between marketing and dating began to intrigue me years ago. In my career field, we understand that the *Field of Dreams* technique for branding doesn't usually work. The changing landscape means we need new strategies.

Sadly, most people enter the dating pool with a "love will find a way" mindset. I see tremendously talented people make smart decisions in their industries, but when it comes to love, they end up winging it. People spend more time thinking through their next car purchase than they do dating. The decision of a lifelong mate is too big to leave to chance.

The more I explored the connection between branding and dating, the more I realized the principles that brands use to rise to the top could prove instrumental in helping men and women hit the mark. I believe this six-part strategy is more than a mere system. It's a movement that can empower people to not only meet the loves of their lives but also create relationships that thrive.

Brands develop marketing tactics as they struggle to break through the clutter and noise of the growing number of products available daily. Individuals face a similar challenge in the modern dating marketplace. No longer is the dating pool limited to our neighborhood, church, or school. With the internet in our pocket, the number of potential relationships has grown to include the entire world. Options, competition, and rising expectations make it more complicated than ever for brands to find their target audience. And those same aspects complicate the way we navigate love.

Part of the problem lies in the myriad ways people view love. Too many see it as a feeling, something fleeting and temporary. But I want more for you than this Hollywood sense of love. I believe it can be bigger than a quickened heartbeat or a prince rescuing a damsel and riding off into the sunset.

Brands work hard to build loyalty and lasting collaborations. They want people to "love" their products so much they become devoted customers. My passion is to encourage people to see love for another person in much the same way—as a purposeful, sustainable connection. I call this the real happily ever after. Love should be a partnership where both people grow, while they support and challenge each other to be the best versions of themselves.

## Defining Love

Before we go any further with this discussion of love, it's vital that we understand the basics of the verb. Chances are, someone in your past has told you, "I love you." It might have been a parent, a friend, a partner, or even a stranger in passing. But what did they mean by that? Take a moment to think about it. What did the person actually mean when they said those words?

Truthfully, no matter how universal the phrase "I love you" might seem, everyone interprets it differently. What the person meant may or may not align with what you understood it to mean. This is one of the greatest challenges in relationships. Every person's imprint brings with it a different definition of love.

Other languages give relationships a bit of an edge. For example, in Spanish, "te encanto" or "te quiero" are phrases you might tell your parents or friends. You might even say, "me encanta" about chocolate. On the other hand, "te amo" goes much deeper. These are words reserved for a romantic and lasting love.

But even in Greek, Spanish, Italian, and French, without a shared understanding regarding these different types of love, we can misinterpret, miscommunicate, and ultimately miss out on what love truly is.

So, let's fix that. Let's establish a standard definition of love—one that will serve as our foundation throughout this book. Erich Fromm narrowed love down to four key components. Understanding them will help you recognize real love when it's present, and just as importantly, know when it's not.

After years of studying philosophy, religion, psychology, and the lived experiences of people around the world, I've come to believe the four components Erich Fromm outlined in *The Art of Loving* provide a tremendous definition.

Fromm presented knowledge, care, respect, and responsibility as the core concepts of love. These aren't just abstract ideas; they are actionable proof points. If one or more of these is missing, then it's not truly love. As M. Scott Peck explained, "The will to extend one's self for the purpose of nurturing one's own or another's spiritual growth." Let me paint a picture with a simple analogy.

Imagine you have a plant, and you tell people you love it. Proof of that love is found in those four actionable steps.

- **Knowledge**—Love knows how to help the beloved thrive. In the plant analogy, you would know if your plant needs water, sunlight, or a certain type of soil. If you don't know the plant's basic needs, how can you claim to love it?
- **Care**—Knowing isn't enough; love actively cares as well. If you know your plant needs water but don't take time to tend to it, your inaction proves your love is incomplete.

- **Respect**—Respect means recognizing and honoring the other's unique nature. Love isn't about imposing your desires; it's about meeting the other's needs in a way that honors their individuality. If you pour alcohol on the plant instead of water because that's what *you* prefer, you're not respecting what the plant truly needs.
- **Responsibility**—Finally, love requires responsibility; it takes ownership of caring for the beloved. If you go on vacation for five weeks and leave the plant unattended, no amount of prior knowledge, care, or respect can compensate for neglecting your responsibility.

Now, let's bring this analogy back to relationships. If someone says they love you but don't truly know your dreams, fears, and what makes you unique, how can it be real love? If they know you but don't actively show up for you emotionally or physically, can they honestly claim to love you? Are they truly loving you if they care for you but don't honor your boundaries, preferences, or individuality? And if they know you, care for you, and respect you, but don't take responsibility for nurturing the relationship, is what they feel really love? Love isn't just a feeling or a word; it's an action, or a series of actions, rooted in knowledge, care, respect, and responsibility.

When my wife and I were preparing for marriage, we had a conversation about the phrase "I love you." We recognized that when we spoke those words with authenticity, they could be substituted with, "I'm all FOUR you." In other words, "I know you, I care for you, I respect you, and I am responsible for you." If any one of these four components is missing, then love is incomplete. I hope you will, like me, think of this whenever you hear ANYONE say "I love you." Is it love FOUR real? Are they declaring "All FOUR" love[IP]?

# ALL "FOUR" LOVE

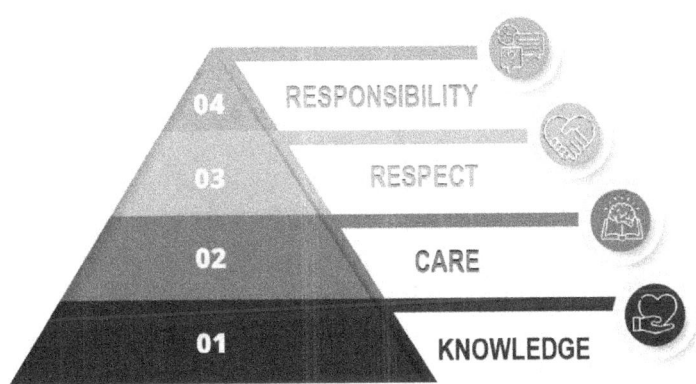

This definition of love gave us a shared foundation, a common platform to build our relationship. And it will give you and me a cooperative definition as we walk together through these pages. But even with the definition in place, the questions remain: How do we get to that place? How can we find that kind of commitment? What can we do to achieve happily ever after forever?

## Reframe Our Thinking

The key lies in reframing our thinking. In brand management, we always start with a clear vision of success and then reverse engineer the steps to achieve it. We begin with the end in mind, but first, we might have to redefine the end.

When most people think about relationships, they often picture the wedding day as the grand finale. It's the moment we've been conditioned to see as the ultimate goal, the triumphant "happily ever after." After all, Cinderella marries Prince Charming, and Tiana weds Naveen. The end. Roll Credits. Right?

But I want to challenge that perspective. I believe the wedding day is not the end. Rather, it's the beginning. When I worked at Facebook, which had already been growing as a company for fifteen years, they had a very true and motivating phrase, "We are only 1 percent done."

The same is true for a lifelong relationship. The real challenge and true growth come when you develop a sustaining love, a deeper connection. Success in a relationship means building a fulfilling, enduring partnership. My desire is for you to view love as more than idealistic notions or passing feelings. I want you to see it as strategic, intentional, and long-lasting.

To start at the end, we have to consider:

- What will my ideal relationship look like in ten years?
- In twenty years?
- In forty years?
- What kind of life, love, and legacy do I want to build?

After you truthfully answer those questions, you can begin to make choices and develop strategies that will take you to that purposeful end.

Love and relationships can seem slippery and uncertain. And while there are no guarantees in life or in marketing, we can do a few things to increase our likelihood of success and give us more confidence. So, let's get started. Whether you're in the earliest stages of dating, preparing for a commitment, or navigating the challenges of a relationship, I want to help you take the spirit of marketing and apply it to the most important "brand" any of us will ever build: our lives.

## Take Action

Let's start at the end and answer those questions we framed earlier. Whether you're in a relationship or not, the best time to start thinking about these things is now. Don't worry about getting them perfect just yet. As you work through the 6 Ps Platform[IP], you may need to come back and rewrite these answers. But go ahead and be honest because you can't move forward until you know where you're going.

1. What will my ideal relationship look like in ten years?
_____
_____
_____
_____

2. In twenty years?
_____
_____
_____
_____

3. In forty years?
_____
_____
_____
_____

4. What kind of life, love, and legacy do I want to build?

___

5. How does the definition of love—knowledge, care, respect, and responsibility—compare to the way you've viewed love in the past?

___

# CHAPTER TWO

# Understanding the Paradigm Shift

*Freedom of choice is also freedom to decide when you do not want to choose.*

—attributed to Simona Botti

*Oh, it's slim pickins*
*If I can't have the one I love, I guess it's you that I'll be kissin'*
*Just to get my fixins*
*Since the good ones are deceased or taken*
*I'll just keep on moanin' and bitchin'*

—From the song "Slim Pickens" by Sabrina Carpenter

The dating landscape has changed drastically over the last one hundred years. Prior to the nineteenth century, arranged marriages were common. The idea of romantic love is actually a modern luxury. Tribal customs and royal alliances meant marriage was based on strategy rather than compatibility. Even through the 1940s and 50s, most American marriages were based on proximity, duty, or survival instead of emotional freedom.

It wasn't until the last half of the twentieth century that things began to change. The women's liberation movement and the sexual revolution pushed cultural norms, and individuals began to have more freedom to choose. Options were only limited by social circles and cities. You couldn't date who you didn't know!

The technological age increased the dating pool exponentially. Social media, dating apps, and more freedom to travel globally opened the door to almost endless possibilities. The only thing holding people back was cultural and religious constraints. People allowed family pressures and stereotypes to narrow their options.

In the last decade or two, we've moved into a brand new "Era of Dating Autonomy." We have full freedom and access. With a wide-open, swipe-driven dating scene, the paradox has flipped. Instead of the immensely limited field our ancestors experienced, we now face an overabundance of options. The shelves are fuller than ever before.

## The Crowded Shelf

Up until the 1990s, shelves were reserved for real stores and catalogs, and each one could only hold so many items. However, with each revolution throughout history—industrial, social, and digital—humans have seen a bit more freedom, and we've watched our options grow at a parallel rate. No longer are we limited to the choices at the general store or the small dating pool at the church social.

On today's internet shelves—the physical or digital spaces where products compete for attention—we find big brands, small startups, influencer-led ventures, and niche offerings all vying for consumer dollars. This mirrors the dating world,

## Understanding the Paradigm Shift

where the number of potential partners is larger than ever, thanks to apps, global travel, and digital communication.

This explosion of choices and opportunities has created many difficulties as well. Marketers call it decision fatigue or analysis paralysis. People either become overwhelmed and make no choice at all, or they make choices based on superficial factors.

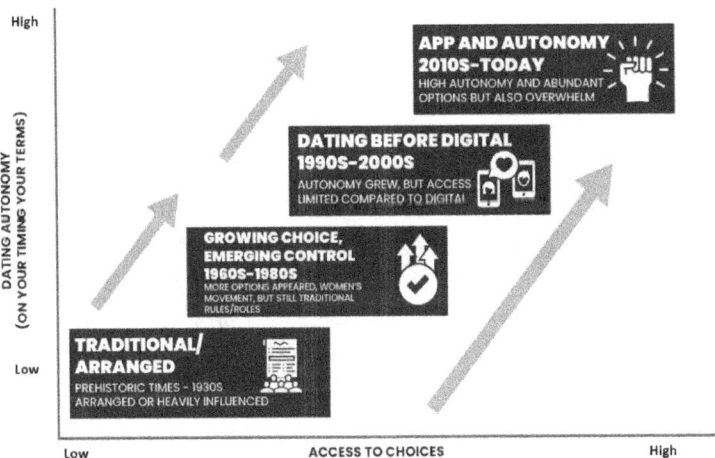

Digital tools provide increased accessibility, convenience, and efficiency, albeit at the cost of some traditional social structures. With the growth of dating apps and people's expectations and hesitations rising daily, successful relationships require adaptation. You can best navigate this crowded, fast-paced landscape by adopting a marketer's mindset.

Marketers recognize the complexities in the crowded shelf marketplace. Instead of allowing the competitive nature of their world to overwhelm them, successful teams develop strategies that put their products or services in front of the right consumers. This same shift in thinking can give today's prospective daters an edge by narrowing the immense field. That's what we do when we learn to Date Like a Brand.

## You Don't Have to Sell Yourself

Before we go any further, I think it's important to understand the nature of marketing. When people hear the phrase *Date Like a Brand,* some imagine I want them to learn how to sell themselves. But nothing could be further from the truth. I'm not in the business of selling; I'm in the profession of marketing.

By becoming aware of the dating marketplace, you can be strategic about how you present yourself and where you invest your time and energy. You can learn how to market yourself. We need to develop a mindset that pushes us to focus on finding someone who appreciates our unique qualities.

Remember, Dating Like a Brand is marketing, not selling. If you have to sell yourself, you're already on the defensive. Selling is transactional. It's short-term. It's about the moment. And unfortunately, many of those books you'll find in the relationship aisle are thinly disguised sales manuals. They give you tactics, pick-up lines, and persuasion techniques. Those books want to teach you how to pitch yourself so you can "close the deal."

Marketing is different. It's transformational. It's long-term. It's about positioning your value so clearly that the right people seek you out.

I was trained at the company that invented brand management. We didn't chase shelf space; we created demand. We didn't just pitch products; we built brands. The best brands never have to beg. They just show up clearly and consistently. Their authenticity attracts the right consumers.

## Understanding the Paradigm Shift

I don't want to help you find someone to buy you. My goal is to help you become a person people buy into. And that's a massive difference. "Buying you" is a moment based on surface value, attraction, or even scarcity. "Buying into you" is a journey. It requires truth, resonance, trust, and alignment. It's deeper than charm. It's built on clarity. And it's what real connection—the kind that lasts—is made of.

Let's look at some of the biggest differences between Selling and Marketing.

| Selling | vs | Marketing |
|---|---|---|
| You convince buyers | | You attract the right customer |
| You close the deal | | You build long-term demand |
| Someone chooses you | | You become the obvious choice |
| Someone buys you | | Someone buys into you |
| Is transactional | | Is transformational |

Marketing is about becoming a brand someone can believe in—not just date for the weekend. It means you no longer pitch yourself; you authentically position yourself.

Brands that embrace authenticity soon discover it's their greatest asset. Consumers look for the truth. In the same way, you will attract people when you are genuine about who you are. Being real allows us to cut through the noise and find people who align with our values.

This authenticity also creates a foundation for brand loyalty. Meaningful connections build strong relationships. When we focus on depth rather than quantity, we may find ourselves with fewer dates, but rather than quick interactions, we end up with strong relationships.

## You Are a Brand

The relationship changes and technology trends of the last twenty years emphasize the importance of understanding the current dating landscape as a "marketplace" with its own rules, driven by technological advances and shifting societal norms. We have to begin to look at ourselves differently and take in the world from a different perspective.

In his book *The E-Mind*, Kary Oberbrunner recommends that everyone look at themselves as a brand. He writes to entrepreneurs, but he invites every person to act like they are trying to market themselves when they apply for a job. I take his premise one step further—we need to become aware of our brand as we date, so we can sift through the wrong matches, recognize the right one, and build momentum towards a strong commitment.

I understand most people reading this book aren't marketers. You probably don't have an MBA, and honestly, you might not care much about marketing at all. But to get the most out of what's ahead, I need you to temporarily set that aside and adopt a new mindset. You are a brand, and you are your own brand manager. Whether you realize it or not, you're already navigating a competitive marketplace—the dating world—and the principles of marketing can give you the tools to compete strategically.

But here's the twist: you're not the only brand in this story. Somewhere out there is another person, another brand, also doing the inner work, clarifying their value, strengthening their proposition, and managing their own growth. Your goal isn't just to improve your brand in isolation. It's to ultimately find a partner brand, someone whose value

# Understanding the Paradigm Shift

proposition complements yours and whose timing aligns, so the two of you can come together and co-launch a relationship built on loyalty, mutual growth, and shared vision.

Think of yourself as the CEO of You, crafting and executing a strategy to stand out, while also identifying the right co-founder to build something lasting.

To that end, I've developed the 6 Ps Platform inspired by brand management. Each step builds on the last to create a strategic path toward a thriving relationship. In the following pages, I'll show you how the marketing world uses the 6 Ps Platform.

1. **Pre-Assessment**—Before launching, marketers identify trends, opportunities, and threats to navigate the space strategically. Dating requires the same understanding of your own brand, who you seek in a partner, and the market itself before you dive in.

2. **Purpose**—You've probably heard the phrase "Define Your Why" from Simon Sinek. We can't skip this critical step if we want to move forward in the dating realm.

3. **Positioning**—Marketers understand the need to accurately identify the things that make their product or service unique. Unfortunately, few in the dating world have truly defined their unique brand proposition.

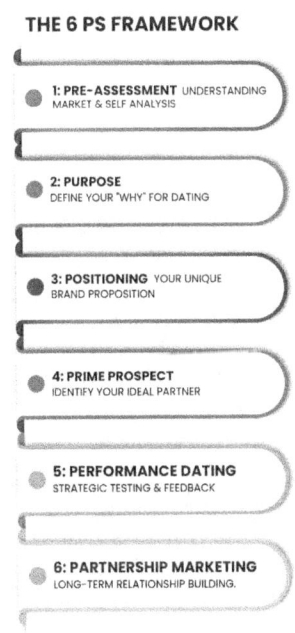

THE 6 PS FRAMEWORK

1: PRE-ASSESSMENT UNDERSTANDING MARKET & SELF ANALYSIS

2: PURPOSE DEFINE YOUR "WHY" FOR DATING

3: POSITIONING YOUR UNIQUE BRAND PROPOSITION

4: PRIME PROSPECT IDENTIFY YOUR IDEAL PARTNER

5: PERFORMANCE DATING STRATEGIC TESTING & FEEDBACK

6: PARTNERSHIP MARKETING LONG-TERM RELATIONSHIP BUILDING.

4. **Prime Prospect Identification**—Marketers do not market to everyone; we target the people who will be the most likely to purchase our product or service and who will be most valuable over time. By focusing on key Prime Prospect Partners (PPPs), we set ourselves up to succeed.
5. **Performance Dating**—In marketing, "launching" isn't guesswork—it's about testing, learning, and adjusting based on real-world feedback. Dating should work the same way. This phase is where you take your strategy into the world, try your fit with different "Partner Brands," and ultimately set up a sustaining relationship launch.
6. **Partnership Marketing**—A wedding or long-term commitment isn't the finish line; it's the beginning of an entirely new journey. Just like brands co-create campaigns, solve challenges together, and evolve over time, strong couples must continue investing, communicating, and adapting. Successful partnerships are built on shared vision, mutual effort, ongoing collaboration—and hopefully leaving a legacy.

We'll explore how each of these steps can give you an advantage as you look for Mr. or Mrs. Right and build your relationship to make it last long beyond the day you say, "I do."

The best relationships aren't found by luck. They're built through intention and understanding. The future of dating means love isn't left to chance. Instead, I want to give your heart a tremendous marketing plan!

And the good news is, even if you don't find your perfect match, you'll be a better person, more equipped to handle life and recognize the best personal life positions when they present themselves.

## Take Action

Assess yourself. Are you currently selling or marketing?

1. Are you trying to convince someone you're the right person to date, or are you attracting the right partners?

   _____

   _____

2. Are you trying to close the deal with every date, or are you looking for long-term demand?

   _____

   _____

3. Are you hoping someone chooses you, or have you made yourself into the obvious choice?

   _____

   _____

4. Do you want someone to buy you (hang out with you), or are you looking for someone who buys into you (understands and believes in you)?

   _____

   _____

5. Do you want a relationship that leaves you exactly where you are in life, or would you prefer a relationship that makes you the best form of yourself?

   _____

   _____

6. Which side of each question would you prefer to be on?
_____
_____

# PART TWO
## BRAND PLANNING

# CHAPTER THREE

# Pre-Assessment, Part One

*You can plan a pretty picnic.*
*But you can't predict the weather*
—From "Ms. Jackson" by Outkast

Marketers don't just launch a new brand blindly. They study the market, their competitors, cultural shifts, and consumer behaviors to understand the landscape and the way it is changing. Pre-assessment helps them identify trends, opportunities, and threats—so they can navigate the space strategically.

Dating works the same way. When we compare today's landscape to the scene ten, twenty, or fifty years ago, the difference is significant. Too many people make dating decisions in a vacuum. They assume their experience is personal rather than part of a larger wave of biological, social, cultural, and economic shifts.

With all the transitions, we need to assess the way these areas impact our dating experience. When was the last time you asked how technology, culture, and societal changes have reshaped the way we connect? In order to succeed, we have to recognize the benefits and pitfalls of apps, introductions, long-distance connections, and social media.

It's essential to compare today's dating norms to the past and draw parallels to the challenges marketers face in today's crowded marketplace. Additionally, it's vital to take a step back and honestly look at our own mindsets, biases, and patterns.

Ask yourself some questions as you evaluate the factors that shape the dating world and especially our approach.

- What external agents play into the dating world today?
- What personal experiences shape my dating approach?

Plus, we want to know where we've come from and where we're going. When my team begins to pre-assess the market for a new product, I encourage them to approach the research with three types of sight:

- **Hindsight**—Using clues from the past that continue to influence the present
- **Insight**—Understanding what is in front of you or what is "in sight." Looking at the current market and consumer dynamics in a deep way
- **Foresight**—Utilizing the knowledge you acquire to optimize future results and developing a vision to walk into that future with confidence

This same triad can provide amazing clarity for your dating perspective.

When we pre-assess to define the landscape, there are two critical components we need to focus on. The Two Cs of the Dating Market are the Category and the Consumer. Diving deep into each allows us to understand what we're walking into and prepare ourselves for the best possible outcome.

Pre-Assessment, Part One

## The Deep Dive Into the Category

When we begin to talk about the category of dating, hindsight shows us that the term dating first showed up in 1896 when a columnist, referring to dates in a girlfriend's diary that were filled by plans with other guys, noted: "I s'pose the other boy's fillin' all my dates.[3] Prior to that, courtship ruled, and while the 1700s invited a bit of romance into the picture, several cultural norms led the way:

- **Religious Rules** defined moral standards and responsibilities within a marriage.
- **Economic Shifts** meant marriage was used to secure wealth and power.
- **Social Hierarchies** caused families to dictate "acceptable" partners.
- **Political Strategies** were the focus of alliances among powerful families.

You might say that mating rather than dating was the norm.

However, unlike animals, which get together purely for reproduction, humans have always needed a bigger connection. Fortunately, the dynamic duo of hormones helps create a bond that goes deeper than any contract written by desperate parents.

When we start interacting with a potential partner, inside jokes, eating together, and spending time with one another trigger dopamine release. This is the brain's "happy juice." It makes you feel awesome and keeps you coming back to the object of your affection. Intimate moments release dopamine's partner, oxytocin. "The cuddle hormone," oxytocin strengthens the bonds as well. You might call it nature's super glue for relationships.

These hormones are at the root of romantic relationships. This biology fosters emotional commitment and continues to shape our relationships today. It drives us to crave long-term commitment, deep emotional connections, and teamwork. Love is more than just some social construct. It's part of our biology.

When love was more mating than dating, it was bigger than a mere emotional experience. It was a survival tool. The goal was not personal fulfillment, but rather biological success. Love gave humans an advantage over other species by promoting long-term partnerships and stability. Like any great product innovation, love solved multiple problems.

- ☑ Love created stable pairing bonds for raising children.
- ☑ Love encouraged emotional attachment, which ensured caregiving.
- ☑ Love enabled cooperation and resource sharing between families.
- ☑ Love laid the foundation for complex social structures like villages, communities, and civilizations.

The early days of commerce looked like this dating paradigm. Functionality ruled the marketing sphere. Branding wasn't really a thing. Products were designed out of need—soap to clean, food to eat, and tools to work. But with each social and technological shift, the picture changed. And with those moves, brands began to differentiate themselves in ways that connected to emotions rather than needs.

During the "functional" eras of dating, love was optional, and partnership was the priority. The same technological and social shifts that changed the marketing world also disrupted the dating scene. We now find ourselves in a world with a fluid, ever-changing, and often overwhelming dating experience. To navigate this crowded, fast-paced landscape, we have to recognize the way our category has evolved over the years. The freedoms we've achieved have morphed into a myriad of choices. Understanding the broad spectrum of the category of dating and the natural instincts of humanity will put us in a better position to find success in our dating goals.

## The Deep Dive Into the Consumer

After we understand the category, we have to develop a clear idea about our consumer. Marketers never create products without deeply researching their target audience. In dating, your target audience is whoever you're looking to date.

You'll notice I used the word consumer rather than customer. A customer makes a one-time purchase and moves on. When someone buys a car, they sign the papers and drive off the lot. Unless the dealer has offered to change the oil for free a few times or you have problems with the car, the customer probably won't return.

A consumer goes deeper than a single transaction, and the fundamental truth about dating is that we want more than a one-time transaction as we search for a meaningful relationship. Those dealers who offer oil changes and maintenance build bridges that take their audience from customer to consumer. This type of relationship requires ongoing investment and adjustments. Think of it like a subscription-based service you renew every year as you build trust. A consumer is someone who continues to engage, consume, and feel valued over time, precisely the things we look for in a lasting relationship.

While gender equality is vital in the areas of careers and financial matters, the fact is the typical male consumer is wired just a bit differently than the typical female. Historically, men had just a few straightforward relationship goals: provide, protect, and procreate. More than some cute 1950s marketing slogan, these traits were an evolutionary imperative. A woman or her guardian—the person responsible for finding her a mate—looked for key biological and social needs. They wanted a man who could ensure survival and security in unstable times, as well as social status and a legacy.

Men also put more emphasis on physical indicators of fertility and youth. Hello, evolutionary psychology! But as society, economics, and culture evolved, so did the expectations and desires of men and women in relationships. Changes in the first thousand years of dating, as in marketing, were barely noticeable. However, things have morphed so much in the last hundred years, ancient worlds wouldn't recognize it.

| The Shifting Dating Priorities Throughout the Generations | | | |
|---|---|---|---|
| Generation | Men Valued | Women Valued | What Dating Was Like |
| Traditional born 1922-1945 | Loyal, dependable wife who managed the household | Strong, financially stable man who could provide | A Job Interview. Not looking for passion, but qualifications |
| Boomers born 1946-1964 | Mix of tradition and emotional connection | Stability was key with the added hope of love and partnership | A Well-Crafted TV Commercial. Structured, but with charm and romance |

## Pre-Assessment, Part One

| Generation | Men Valued | Women Valued | What Dating Was Like |
|---|---|---|---|
| X born 1965-1980 | Committed but independent partner. Less traditional | Equality. Career and ambition as well as attraction | A Competitive Job Market. Prove you are a well-rounded package |
| Millennials born 1981-1996 | Authenticity, emotional intelligence, shared experience | A partner who supported their ambitions | A Tech Start-Up Pitch. You needed a vision, mission, and proof of long-term potential |
| Z born 1997-2012 | Mental Wellness, self-expression, and partners who align with their lifestyle | Deep connection, communication, and respect of her independence | An Online Subscription. Everything is customizable and can be cancelled |

The Shifting Dating Priorities Throughout the Generations

## What This Means for Dating Consumers in the 21st Century

All these changes mean men and women today have more choices than ever before. They also add significant complexity and confusion to the dating scene. When we compare the pros and the cons of these changes, it can help us understand the Category and the Consumers a bit better.

## Modern Dating Challenges for Men

- ✗ **Loss of the "default provider" role**
  With women able to provide for themselves, men can't rely on financial status alone.
- ✗ **Unclear dating norms**
  Traditional chivalry is questioned, and relationship roles have become fluid.
- ✗ **Emotional intelligence is a requirement, not a bonus**
  Men who struggle with vulnerability and communication may find themselves at a disadvantage.

## The Good News

- ✓ **Men can focus on more than just providing**
  Emotional connection, shared values, and personality matter more than ever.
- ✓ **More room for individuality**
  No need to fit into a rigid role; each man can define a "good partner."
- ✓ **Women now prioritize compatibility**
  The best relationships today are based on shared goals, not outdated roles.

## Modern Dating Challenges for Women

- ✗ **More options, but less certainty**
  The paradox of choice makes it harder to feel confident in decisions.
- ✗ **The rise of "situationships"**
  More casual relationships mean women must work harder to find long-term commitment.
- ✗ **Emotional labor**
  Women are often expected to be the emotionally intelligent partner, which can be exhausting.

## The Good News

- ✓ **Women have more freedom than ever before**
  They are no longer forced into relationships out of necessity.
- ✓ **Emphasis on compatibility over financial stability**
  Love is increasingly about shared values, lifestyles, and emotional support.
- ✓ **More autonomy and a greater ability to define what they want**
  Women now have the tools to curate their dating experience like never before.

Marketing has run parallel to dating throughout the ages. When dating moved from dependable qualities to emotions, marketing shifted from building a good product for the Traditional Generation to an era of emotional branding for the Boomers. Generation X watched brands like Nike and Apple sell a lifestyle with their products and expected a well-rounded lifestyle in their dates.

## Marketing to the Access Generation

This means that as we move forward, we have to understand which brands Millennials and Generation Z are supporting. Gen Z, in particular, has grown up in a world where ownership is optional and access is everything. Why build a library when you can stream? Why buy a car when you can Uber? Why commit to a mortgage when Airbnb gives you the world on demand?

This mindset, rooted in flexibility, customization, and cost-efficiency, has quietly made its way into relationships. Many aren't looking to "own" love. They're streaming it. This generation tends to look at relationships more like subscriptions with no upfront cost, free cancellation, low commitment, and constant options. Unfortunately, while streaming works great for music, it's less effective for building something that will last a lifetime.

## LOVE MINDSET SHIFT
## RENT VS. OWN

| PRIORITIZES FLEXIBILITY | PRIORITIZES COMMITMENT |
|---|---|
| **ACCESS-BASED (RENTING)** | **OWNERSHIP-BASED (BUYING)** |
| • High Flexibility | • High Commitment |
| • Low Commitment | • Less Flexibility |
| • Cancel Anytime | • Long-term investment |
| • Constant options | • Emotional Security |

## DATE LIKE A BRAND

That's why today's market feels so volatile. People want the benefits of love—companionship, connection, and fun—without the buy-in. But just like with any brand, if people aren't invested, they'll scroll past you the moment something shinier pops up. It's vital for those in this generation, as well as the ones marketing to them, that you consider the possible dangers of relegating love to the realm of subscriptions.

Pre-Assessment, Part One

## Assessing the VUCA of the Dating Scene

One of the most basic forms of assessment in marketing also works well for navigating the dating landscape. It's a set of criteria that the military reduced to the acronym VUCA.

Originally coined to describe the unpredictable environments in warfare, VUCA perfectly encapsulates the Volatility, Uncertainty, Complexity, and Ambiguity at play in the marketing and dating landscapes today.

As I've pointed out, the dating world has undergone seismic shifts over the past few decades. One conversation with my father before he passed crystallized just how much things have changed in a single generation.

I asked my Dad why he got married when he did (he was twenty-six). He, of course, said my mom was amazing, and then he said, "And, how else was I going to have sex?"

The rise of online dating apps, the normalization of casual hookups, and the proliferation of social media platforms have created an environment where the rules of engagement are constantly evolving. One moment, a new app dominates the scene, and the next, an emerging trend like "soft ghosting" or "situationships" becomes the norm. This constant flux mirrors the difficulties marketers face as consumer preferences shift with the speed of a viral TikTok trend.

- **Volatility** in dating occurs when the sheer volume of potential matches, trends like "breadcrumbing" or "zombie-ing," and the speed of connection and rejection on apps create emotional highs and lows and leave singles feeling overwhelmed.
- **Uncertainty** reigns supreme in dating as well as life. Marketers can't predict whether their current campaign will resonate with their audience or fall flat. Likewise, a swipe on a dating app may match you with someone, but it's hard to discern their true intentions.

Are they looking for a long-term relationship or just a casual fling? Without a clear dating strategy that allows us to filter out distractions and focus on meaningful connections, we can easily experience confusion about a potential partner's intentions, have difficulty gauging whether a connection will lead to something meaningful, and allow fear to make the wrong choice among seemingly endless options.

- **Complexity** in dating stems from multiple intersecting factors like cultural diversity, individual preferences, and societal pressures. Just as marketers must navigate intricate consumer demographics and psychographics, daters must grapple with varying relationship goals, communication styles, and compatibility factors. The diversity of platforms, each catering to different types of connections, balancing the demands of career, family, and personal growth while dating, and understanding how factors like age, values, and life goals intersect with attraction, all play into the complex environment.
- **Ambiguity** is perhaps the most challenging aspect of the dating and marketing landscapes. Marketers often face ambiguous feedback when interpreting data or predicting consumer behavior.

In dating, mixed messages top the list of things that add to the vague nature of relationships. People say one thing, but their actions don't align. For instance, they show interest but never commit. This may stem from undefined relationships. What does it mean to be "dating," "talking," "going out," or being "exclusive"? These ambiguous status descriptions and the equally uncertain expectations that accompany them cause misunderstandings. And the differing communication styles leave many singles confused about where they stand.

## Pre-Assessment, Part One

Marketers navigate VUCA markets by developing strategies that combat these elements. Without a plan, the chaos makes it easy to feel lost or overwhelmed. Today's dating world is undeniably VUCA—Volatile, Uncertain, Complex, and Ambiguous. By adopting strategic marketing principles, singles can head into the chaos with confidence, turning challenges into opportunities for meaningful connection.

Just as great brands succeed by differentiating themselves and staying true to their purpose, you too can find success in love by bringing clarity, focus, and intentionality to the Category and Consumers you'll face on your dating journey. That's what makes this pre-assessment so vital.

## Take Action

Before we move forward, take a moment to look at your current situation. Consider these areas of impact so you can build on them as we continue.

1. How has the changing landscape made things more or less complicated in your personal dating experience?

_____
_____
_____

2. Look at the VUCA in your immediate dating landscape. What volatility do you see?

_____
_____
_____

3. How do you feel about the uncertainty in the current dating atmosphere?

_____
_____
_____

4. Where have you seen complexities arise in your personal dating space?

_____
_____
_____

5. When have you faced ambiguity in past relationships, and what would be the best means to avoid this in the future?

_____
_____
_____

# CHAPTER FOUR

# Pre-Assessment Part Two

*And deep in my heart, the answer, it was in me*
*And I made up my mind to define my own destiny*
—From "The Miseducation of Lauryn Hill" by Lauryn Hill

Now that we understand the market variables—in our search for the ideal partner, we'll call it the dating landscape—it's time to pre-assess the product. You! Every great brand begins with a strong foundation: a set of beliefs and values that guide its actions and identity. Before you can consider dating, relationships, or finding the love of your life, you have to understand yourself.

As my long-time mentor, Mark Pritchard, often says, "The fruits are in the roots." This principle is a universal truth, applying as much to the world of branding as it does to our personal lives. To cultivate a thriving relationship, you must first dig deep into where you came from. Just like any brand must understand its origins and purpose, you must understand the foundation upon which your life is built. Who you are today, the choices you make, and the relationships you pursue are deeply connected to the bedrock laid for you in your early years.

## The Fruits Are in the Roots: Your Brand Foundation

Every brand has a story, and that story starts with its founder. The innovator's vision, values, and experiences shape the brand's identity and direction. Think about Steve Jobs. His obsession with simplicity and innovation became the cornerstone of Apple. Oprah Winfrey's commitment to authenticity and empowerment shaped her media brand. These two brands didn't come out of nowhere. They grew from deeply personal roots.

You are no different. Your story begins with your earliest influences—your parents or caregivers. These adults acted as your first founders. They unknowingly shaped you as a "product" and prepared you for the world.

From the moment you were born, they cultivated your value to the market. This "market value", which we will get into later, is comprised of four elements: Mind, Body, Soul, and Resources. Your parents and teachers nurtured your mind and helped you develop intellect and curiosity. Grandparents and aunts and uncles helped your parents care for your body, ensuring you had the health and strength to grow. Parents, spiritual leaders, and other caring individuals instilled values in your soul, teaching you right from wrong and helping you connect with the world around you. Each person you encountered during your youth laid the groundwork for how you view and care for resources. They taught you what you know about financial literacy, work ethic, and independence.

Though we don't discuss it as a human growth principle, these influential people worked within a premise we call *imprinting*.

## The Relationship Imprint

We hear about imprinting most often in the animal kingdom. Perhaps you've seen cartoons where a duckling hatches and attaches itself to a human or a bear because it's the first thing the little duck sees. Instead of learning to be a duck, the tiny creature takes on the habits of the creature it met first.

In marketing, we use this imprinting concept to understand how consumers develop early associations with a product or category. For instance, if you grew up in a home that used a particular brand of laundry detergent, the scent of that detergent might forever be linked to your idea of "clean." This association is not necessarily objective; it's based on your experience.

The same principle applies to relationships. The people who raised you provided the first and most influential imprint of what a relationship looks like. Whether you grew up in a home with two loving parents, a single parent, or some other family dynamic, you had a front row seat to how people handled conflict and treated one another. These people probably formed your definition of love and commitment.

Regardless of whether their imprint created a positive, healthy reaction to relationships or looked more like a cautionary tale to avoid, the lessons you learned have a subconscious hold on you. Even those who consciously try to move away from their childhood imprint find their subconscious pulling them back to it.

But here's the paradox: many who try to change the cycle created by their childhood imprints end up repeating them. For example, someone who grew up in a home with constant conflict might purposefully seek a peaceful relationship. Yet, they continually find themselves drawn to people who create drama.

This is why self-awareness is so critical. To move forward in our dating journeys, we must understand our imprints.

What messages did you internalize about love, commitment, and partnership? What patterns from your childhood are you unconsciously repeating today?

## Imprints Influence Your Attachment Style

Before we go any further in assessing our imprint, it's imperative to understand that this is not about blaming parents. No one is perfect. Even the most loving and well-meaning parents can unintentionally shape our attachment patterns in ways that seem negative.

Additionally, because they are influenced by all our early interactions, our attachment patterns have their roots in both parents individually, as well as actively involved grandparents, aunts, uncles, nannies, and more. Even older siblings or cousins constantly in the household can make a difference.

Birth order plays a role as well. For instance, the youngest in a family of four siblings may have been raised in a chaotic household with everyone competing for attention, while the firstborn started life in a calmer, more structured environment.

As I mentioned, imprinting has little to do with good or bad parenting. It's about understanding how our earliest connections conditioned us to approach relationships. Recognizing these patterns and how different life circumstances cause each person to make relationship and brand choices gives us the power to make conscious decisions about how we connect, communicate, and love.

Developed by John Bowlby and expanded on by Mary Ainsworth, attachment theory explains how our earliest relationships shape the way we form bonds as adults. As children, we looked to those around us to meet our needs for safety, love, and consistency. Their response to our needs gives us some basic principles to live by. Early in life, we form a set of opinions.

## How We View Life Depending on Our Imprint

|  | One Whose Needs Are Met as a Child | One Whose Needs Are Not Met as a Child |
|---|---|---|
| **Love** | Love is reliable | Love is unpredictable |
| **Emotions** | Emotional needs will be met | Emotional needs will be dismissed |
| **Trust Level** | Others can be trusted | I must protect myself |

These imprinted lessons come from a variety of sources:

- If an older sibling constantly teases or belittles a younger one, that younger child may grow up expecting relationships to include emotional highs and lows.
- If one parent is emotionally warm and nurturing while the other is distant, the child may struggle with mixed expectations of love, sometimes seeking closeness, other times fearing it.

Over time, repeated experiences **create a blueprint** for how we navigate closeness, conflict, and commitment. This blueprint is called our **attachment style**, and it continues to influence our relationships long after childhood.

## Understanding Attachment Styles

An attachment shaped by trust, consistency, and emotional connection sits at the heart of every relationship—whether personal or commercial. In psychology, attachment theory explains how individuals form emotional connections with caregivers and shapes how they approach relationships in adulthood. In marketing, consumer-brand relationships operate on a similar principle: people attach to brands that provide security and reliability and touch them emotionally.

The most fundamental element as we develop relationships is the Trust Factor. This is the core of attachment in life and business. Children learn trust when their caregivers provide consistent love and support. Consumers learn to trust a brand through the reliability of their experiences. When trust is stable, attachment grows stronger. When trust is inconsistent, insecurity follows.

In both cases, we find three key players:

1. The Individual (Child or Consumer)—Expectations, fears, and needs shape their attachment behavior.
2. The Provider (Caregiver or Brand)—Reliability, responsiveness, and consistency build trust.
3. The Relationship (Bond Between the Two)—The level of security that develops over time determines whether the attachment is strong or weak.

Depending on the depth of trust built, relationships fall into one of four primary attachment styles: secure, anxious, avoidant, and disorganized. The attachment style you develop as you grow shapes your behavior, both in the way you relate to brands and one another.

## The Secure Attachment Style

The **Secure Attachment Style** has its roots in loyalty. When children learn that relationships are safe and dependable and believe their caregivers consistently meet their needs, it allows them to trust love itself, even more than just a specific person. Children with this style usually grew up with healthy sibling dynamics and a balance between love and competition.

## Pre-Assessment Part Two

For example, when a child falls off his bike, his mom or dad will likely come and comfort him. His siblings might laugh a little, but it won't be long before they begin to help their fallen sibling. Mom or Dad encourages the rider to get up and try again, and the child feels supported in the midst of laughter and teasing. The ordeal builds trust and security, and as the child grows, he begins to believe in the safety and reliability of relationships. Children raised in this environment become securely attached adults comfortable with intimacy, trust, and long-term commitment.

### How This Shows Up in Relationships:

- They trust their partners and don't need constant reassurance.
- They are emotionally available without being overly dependent.
- They can navigate conflicts without fear of abandonment.

### How This Shows Up in Branding:

- Consumers with secure attachment stick with brands they trust.
- They don't panic over small product changes or brand evolution.
- They tend to form lifelong brand loyalty (e.g., devoted Apple users).

Secure attachments lead to balanced, emotionally fulfilling partnerships where trust and connection grow naturally. Those with this attachment style will need to learn to be patient with those who have different attachment experiences. It's easy to get frustrated with those who are anxious, insecure, or disorganized when you have lived in a more balanced environment.

In branding, secure attachments occur by consistently building trust, and this leads to long-term consumer loyalty.

## The Anxious Attachment Style

The **Anxious Attachment Style** presents itself with needy partners and clingy consumers. Inconsistent caregivers with their sometimes loving, sometimes distant personalities teach children that love is unpredictable. By the time they reach adulthood, these people have developed a deep-seated fear of abandonment. These individuals often crave intimacy but struggle with self-doubt and emotional insecurity.

Imagine a child who looks to a parent for comfort after a bad day at school. One day, she is greeted with hugs and reassurance, but the next, the parent seems distracted and dismissive. At the same time, her sibling provides support one day and comes across as tremendously competitive the next day. The young girl learns to cling to the supportive moments. She longs for love and reassurance, and she fears the thought of those two elements disappearing forever.

### How This Shows Up in Relationships:

- Those with the anxious attachment style seek constant reassurance and validation from partners.
- They may overanalyze small changes in behavior as signs of rejection.
- They can become emotionally overwhelmed, fearing their partner will leave.

## How This Shows Up in Branding:

- Anxious consumers need frequent engagement and reassurance from brands.
- Price changes or product updates may make them fear betrayal.
- They may idealize a brand but turn against it if they feel disappointed.

Sadly, anxiously attached individuals struggle with their self-worth, and too often, they unintentionally push partners away by seeking too much reassurance. They mistake emotional highs for love. If they can learn to self-soothe and trust in love, it can help them build stronger connections. Brands must communicate stability to retain these customers who face insecurity.

## The Avoidant Attachment Style

The **Avoidant Attachment Style** is characterized by distant partners and independent consumers. Avoidant attachment forms when caregivers become emotionally unavailable or dismissive. The child learns to rely only on themselves and ends up having a hard time with emotional intimacy in adulthood. Because self-reliance equals security for these individuals, they may enjoy relationships but resist deep dependence on others.

This attachment style develops when a child feels unsupported by one parent and overly supported by another. For example, when a child gets a bad grade, one parent shrugs it off while the other micromanages their homework so they can do better next time, and it sends mixed signals. The tension between a lack of support and hovering will cause the child to withdraw emotionally and value independence.

### How This Shows Up in Relationships:

- They keep emotional distance, fearing vulnerability.
- They may pull away when a relationship becomes too intimate.
- They often prioritize independence over connection.

### How This Shows Up in Branding:

- Avoidant consumers prefer flexibility and control over commitment.
- They avoid emotional attachment to brands, making them hard to retain.
- They favor transactional interactions (e.g., month-to-month subscriptions rather than long-term commitments).

In relationships, avoidant attachment can lead to emotional disconnect. In order to experience deeper, more fulfilling connections, individuals must learn to embrace vulnerability and trust in relationships. Brands have the tough job of earning trust gradually to convert avoidant consumers into loyal customers.

## The Disorganized Attachment Style

The **Disorganized Attachment Style** creates a conflicted partner or a love-hate consumer. When caregivers become both a source of comfort and fear, the confusion creates a chaotic attachment. Neglect, unpredictability, and harm are tell-tale signs of a childhood destined to develop this style. As adults, these individuals struggle with internal conflict in relationships. They crave and fear intimacy at the same time.

Picture a child who spills a drink. One day, her parent laughs and cleans it up. Another day brings an explosion of anger. One sibling comforts them in the moment; however, later, the spill becomes a weapon in an argument. This child learns that relationships are unpredictable and potentially dangerous.

### How This Shows Up in Relationships:

- Individuals may desire closeness but feel unsafe when they get it.
- Unpredictable emotional responses often accompany this style.
- They may experience cycles of intense love and rejection.

### How This Shows Up in Branding:

- These consumers develop a love-hate relationship with brands, alternating between loyalty and frustration.
- They may express strong emotional reactions to changes in products or policies.
- They struggle with long-term commitment to a brand, switching between competitors.

Disorganized attachment can create a push-pull dynamic in relationships that makes stability difficult. Therapy, self-awareness, and a secure partner can help break this cycle. In branding, mixed signals create conflicted loyalty. Brands must ensure their messaging and actions align consistently to attract consumers with this attachment style.

## Making Your Attachment Style a Strength

After you recognize your attachment style, you can begin to leverage it. Perhaps you've already realized that your attachment tendency impacts who you're drawn to when dating. Spoiler alert! Our attachment styles often push us toward what's familiar, not necessarily a healthy relationship. That means our natural instincts might lead us toward relationships that don't meet our emotional needs.

For example, if you have a Secure Attachment Style, you're probably comfortable with emotional closeness, independence, and healthy communication. You'll be drawn toward people who are emotionally available, consistent, and match your level of openness and trust.

But you'll have to watch out because you might be too understanding of people with anxious or avoidant tendencies. Too often, people in the secure category assume love and patience alone can "fix" unacceptable behaviors in others. While stability can help someone grow, we have to be on the lookout for relationships that feel one-sided—healthy love requires mutual effort.

- ✅ Green Flag for those with a Secure Attachment Style: People who are emotionally available and consistent.
- 🚩 Red Flag for those with a Secure Attachment Style: People whom you think you can "fix."

If you have an Anxious Attachment Style, you'll waver between craving deep connections and the fear of abandonment. Those who have an anxious attachment style find themselves attracted to avoidant partners because their emotional distance triggers the anxious one's need for validation. When a relationship feels "boring" or stable, those with an anxious style might worry that something is missing because they think the emotional highs mean true love. Plus, they'll cling to uncertain relationships even if they don't meet their needs.

## Pre-Assessment Part Two

People with an anxious attachment style need to look for someone who consistently makes them feel secure. Pay attention to how your partner shows up for you, not just how much "chemistry" you feel at the start.

- ✅ Green Flag for those with an Anxious Attachment Style: A partner who reassures you before you ask.
- 🚩 Red Flag for those with an Anxious Attachment Style: A partner who makes you feel like you constantly have to "prove" your worth.

If you have an Avoidant Attachment Style, you value independence and may feel suffocated by too much emotional closeness. This often leads to being attracted to the unavailable. You may look for people with an anxious attachment style because their emotional neediness reinforces your desire to pull away. And secure partners might make you feel uninterested because their consistency doesn't create the emotional "chase" you're used to. You're also more likely to end even great relationships when things get too deep.

Instead of avoiding partners who offer real emotional intimacy, those with the avoidant attachment style should lean into the discomfort of connection and challenge themselves to communicate rather than withdraw.

- ✅ Green Flag for those with an Avoidant Attachment Style: Look for a partner who gives you space but also fosters a deep emotional connection.
- 🚩 Red Flag for those with an Avoidant Attachment Style: A partner who plays emotional games or creates drama—this lets you keep your distance, but it doesn't lead to real love.

Those with a Disorganized Attachment Style often get caught between wanting & fearing love. Relationships feel like a rollercoaster. These individuals frequently jump into intense relationships too quickly, only to sabotage them later because they feel overwhelmed. They attract emotionally unpredictable partners because chaos feels familiar and struggle with trust, pushing people away even when their partner treats them well. Self-awareness and consistency will help heal the person with a disorganized attachment style. Therapy, self-reflection, and surrounding yourself with stable, secure people can help you rebuild trust in love.

- ✅ Green Flag for those with a Disorganized Attachment Style: A partner who provides stability and emotional safety.
- 🚩 Red Flag for those with a Disorganized Attachment Style: A partner who mirrors your past experiences of inconsistency and chaos.

## Your Attachment Style Is Not Set in Stone

Fortunately, adults who recognize their attachment style and the way it developed can redefine the way they attach and imprint. Your past does not have to define your destiny. You may need a therapist or counselor to work through your trust issues and change your perspective on relationships. And it's important to remember, the shift won't happen overnight.

By committing to a healthy relationship and refusing to give up at the first feeling of insecurity, you can learn to trust. You'll need someone dependable, someone who is also committed to building and maximizing their attachment style.

You'll also need to work through the other five Ps so you can better understand your Purpose, Positioning, Performance, and Partnership Plan. Attachment style isn't just about how you interact with brands; it's about how you interact with people. Your attachment style shapes the partners you choose, the dynamics of your relationships, and the way you handle intimacy and trust.

## Take Action

It's time to be honest with yourself. Do you recognize yourself in any of these styles? One of them is very likely influencing your romantic choices. Pre-Assessment may seem tedious. You might be tempted to skip over this important step. However, as you move forward, you'll discover the value of understanding the VUCA of the dating landscape and your own background and attachment style.

1. Who influenced the way you view relationships? Look at each person you list and decide if their example was a positive experience you'd like to replicate or something that would be better to avoid.

    _____
    _____
    _____

2. When you think about your mind, what did the adults in your life impress on you about developing your mind? Did they encourage you to be lifelong learners? Which adults would be best to emulate?

    _____
    _____
    _____

3. How did your childhood affect the way you care for your body? How do you view food and exercise? Do you criticize the way you look?

_____
_____
_____

4. What values and morals did your family impress on your life? After you list them, choose the ones you want to prioritize. Do some values in the list reflect things you want to exclude from your personal list?

_____
_____
_____

5. What resources did the adults in your life provide you with? Do you have a good handle on finances? Did they teach you to view yourself and others with proper respect? What does your career outlook look like? How do you view education?

_____
_____
_____

6. Which attachment style do you recognize in yourself?

_____
_____
_____

## Pre-Assessment Part Two

7. Reflect on how this might be influencing your dating choices.

    Do you seek validation (anxious attachment)?
    Do you push people away (avoidant attachment)?
    Do you feel like you sway between commitment and fear (disorganized attachment)?
    Do you naturally trust relationships until someone proves otherwise (secure attachment)?

8. Could a therapist or a counselor help you develop a secure attachment style?

    _____
    _____
    _____

9. How might your attachment style and the attachment style of people you've connected with have affected your past relationships?

    _____
    _____
    _____

Understanding your attachment style can help you build healthier, more fulfilling connections. Just as brands work to earn consumer trust, you too can create stability and security in your relationships.

Ultimately, the way we attach—whether to people or to brands—boils down to one question: do we trust the bond between us?

# CHAPTER FIVE

# Purpose

*The purpose of life is a life of purpose.*
—Robert Byrne

Simon Sinek's exciting concept, Start with Why, revolutionized the way people approach business and leadership positions. Simple yet profound, the principle explains that when you identify your "why," your actions become intentional, focused, and meaningful. This idea doesn't just apply to businesses or organizations. It's crucial in every part of life, especially dating.

So, now that we understand the Category and Consumer and have identified the VUCA potential in our dating arenas, it's time to be honest about our purpose in dating. Take a minute to consider these three questions to get started:

- Why, exactly, do you choose to put yourself out there?
- What is your endgame?
- Are you looking for companionship, a friend, marriage, or something else entirely?

Defining your end goal is critical. In business and in life, the sharper your vision of success, the better you'll be at charting the path to get there. Without clarity, dating becomes aimless, filled with missteps and wasted time. On the other hand, a clear and honest view of your purpose will align your actions with your vision and ensure you don't waste time or energy on paths that don't serve you.

## What Does Success Look Like?

The most fundamental question for this book is, "Why are you dating in the first place?" Don't be too quick to respond. While the answer might seem obvious, without truly examining our inner selves, we might end up in a place that doesn't feel fulfilling.

Imagine meeting someone who had decided to head west; however, they had never defined their purpose in driving that direction. They might end up in Seattle before they remember they hate the cold and rain. New Mexico, for a person who loves lush forests and gurgling brooks, would be equally awful. Deciding to date without defining success will be just as frustrating as driving toward the Pacific Ocean without a specific destination in mind.

As I mentioned, some look for companionship, love, or connection when they enter the dating arena. Others go so far as to admit they want to start a family. But let's dig deeper. What does success in a relationship look like for you?

If you don't have a clear answer, you're not alone. Many people date without truly understanding their motivations or objectives. They know they're searching for something—a feeling, a person, a future—but without a defined why, how will they know when they've found what they're looking for?

Understanding your why in dating requires another mindset shift. Too many chase the idea of the perfect match or search for someone who checks every box. Instead of defining the why, they focus on the who. However, by shifting your focus to the purpose of a relationship—to grow together, support each other, and build a foundation for a life greater than the sum of its parts—you also define the who.

When you approach dating with this why in mind, it changes everything. You no longer look for someone to complete you or to fit into a preconceived ideal. Instead, you search for someone to partner with, a person who will share life's ups and downs, someone you can help become the best version of themselves while they do the same for you.

## How to Find Love For Your Life

The subtitle of this book promises to provide *A Powerful Framework for Finding and Keeping the Love of Your Life*. Pretty catchy, right? That phrase conjures up visions of the magical "needle in a haystack" moment. You might imagine that somewhere out there, a soulmate waits for you to find them. But here's the truth: that "Love of Your Life" concept is misleading.

The idea of "finding the one" can create a false sense of scarcity and pressure. It implies only one person in the entire world can fulfill the role of forever mate, and you have to find them through some grand romantic journey. While that notion is picturesque, it's not grounded in reality or practicality.

Instead, I want to help you find *love FOR your life*. Notice the difference? It's not about finding the one person you're "destined" to be with. It's about finding someone worthy of partnering with you for all your days, someone who complements your values and growth, and with whom you can build a future.

Thomas Moore, in his book *Soulmates*, defined soulmates not as mystical, preordained partners but as two people who extend themselves for the growth of another. A soulmate relationship isn't about perfection or destiny; it's about effort, intentionality, and mutual commitment.

Using this Platform, the goal of dating is not just to find a spark or a feeling of infatuation. It's to identify someone who can partner with you on the journey of life to build a strong and resilient relationship rooted in mutual growth. Rather than asking, "What can this person give me?" it's time to ask, "How can we build something together?" How would your path change direction if this became your purpose in dating?

Your why will guide you through the dating landscape. It will help you make intentional choices, avoid unnecessary detours, and stay true to what matters most. Without a clear purpose, you might unconsciously date just to have companionship and a good time on the weekends. You may even go into each encounter wondering, "Is this the one?" Unfortunately, using this purposeless mode for dating, you'll probably still be single when you're fifty. It's like throwing darts blindfolded.

## Growing Together

In the business world, brands grow by improving the lives of their customers. For instance, Procter and Gamble's purpose is rooted in making the lives of everyday consumers better. They deliver products that add value, either through convenience, innovation, or quality, to enrich their consumers' lives. The company's commitment fuels loyalty and propels the brand's growth.

P&G's win-win strategy creates a perfect analogy for dating and love. Just as brands grow when they add real value for their consumers, people grow when they find a partner who contributes to their well-being, complements their strengths, and supports their dreams. This dedication inspires reciprocal giving and births a cycle of mutual growth that is sustainable and deeply fulfilling.

How would dating change for you if a big part of your why became growth—personal growth—as well as contributing to the development of another individual? This growth mindset means we stop looking for someone to complete, fix, or serve us. Rather, we search for someone to grow with—a partner equally committed to building something enduring, meaningful, and dynamic.

When both individuals prioritize personal growth and the growth of their relationship, the partnership transcends fleeting attractions or shallow exchanges. They build something rooted in mutual respect, shared goals, and a deep commitment to becoming the best versions of themselves, individually and together.

This mindset shift is the key to finding a relationship that transforms into a thriving partnership. It's about contributing to something greater than yourself while receiving the same in return. When you approach dating and love with this growth mindset, you open the door to finding a partner who not only aligns with your purpose but also propels you toward your highest potential.

## Take Action

Let's take a few minutes to be honest about our journeys. Have you put any thought into what you want from a relationship?

1. Why do you date? It may seem like a ridiculous question. Look at the last few people you've gone out with. Why did you ask them out, or why did you agree to go with them?

   _____
   _____
   _____

2. What three character traits do you want your marriage to have? Consider things like mutual support, growth, and respect, someone who knows me, someone I can know.

   _____
   _____
   _____

3. Which, if any, of the people you've dated in the past year have been able to meet those criteria?

   _____
   _____
   _____

# CHAPTER SIX

# Positioning

> Who am I?
> *Am I who I think I am?*
> AM I ALL THAT I CAN BE?
> —Attributed to Frantz Fanon

Uber boasts it's "the Smartest Way to Get Around. One tap and a car comes directly to you. Your driver knows exactly where to go. And payment is completely cashless." Apple sells iPhones with a simple phrase: "The Experience IS the Product. A phone should be more than a collection of features. A phone should be absolutely simple, beautiful, and magical to use."

Every successful brand has a Unique Selling Proposition (USP)—a clear articulation of the benefits it offers and the reasons to believe in those benefits. The USP defines whatever it is that sets it apart. When they use positioning correctly, it becomes the foundation of why consumers choose their brand over another. A USP might highlight a functional benefit, like a detergent that removes stains better than competitors, or an emotional benefit, like the feeling of confidence that comes from wearing a luxury perfume.

It might even be as simple as an appealing packaging that draws attention on the shelf. Regardless of its form, the USP attracts and retains customers.

## Your Personal USP

Whether we realize it or not, people also have a USP. We present ourselves to others based on certain attributes and benefits, and others assess us in the same way. Defining your USP is vital for dating sites and first introductions. How do you want others to perceive you in those first moments after you meet or before they swipe?

Most USPs focus on the attributes of the brand that are unique or rare, and you can do the same with your personal brand. When we articulate and showcase what makes us special, we become more attractive in the eyes of potential partners.

The easiest way to identify your personal USP is to take an honest look at yourself through the eyes of others.

1. **What do people consistently compliment you on?** Think about things your friends, colleagues, and past partners have commented on. Do they often mention your humor, intellect, empathy, looks, or reliability?
2. **What do you do better than most people?** Perhaps you are an excellent cook or a fantastic listener. Do people call you to solve problems, or do you have more artistic strengths? Part of your USP often lies in natural talents or skills you've honed.
3. **What makes you unique in your social or professional circles?** Consider the ways you stand out in the various groups you belong to. Do you have a rare talent, an unconventional perspective, or an

interesting story? The positive things that make people notice you are part of your USP.

4. **What are you most proud of? What do you value most about yourself?** Perhaps you have an adventurous spirit, or you connect well with others. You might excel academically or in sports. Include these in your USP.

Like the other chapters, you'll find action steps at the end, but take a moment now to answer those four questions and get a head start on your USP. Your USP should highlight your two or three strongest traits, things you already see that are attractive to others. For example, your one or two-sentence USP might sound something like this:

- I'm a natural problem-solver with a quick wit and a passion for adventure.
- I'm a warm, empathetic listener deeply committed to personal growth and connection.

## The Dating Value Proposition

Though first mentioned in the 1940s, the concept of defining a value proposition became a focus in marketing in the late 1980s. With the shelf becoming increasingly crowded, marketers began to home in on their target audience. A luxury brand doesn't target bargain shoppers.

In that same way, people entering the dating realm need to understand their own core values so they can define their ideal partners. Not everyone will be a fit for your value proposition, and that's okay. You don't need to appeal to everyone.

In addition to your USP, each person has a Dating Value Proposition (DVP)[IP]. The USP looks like a headline that grabs attention. Consider some of the most iconic brands.

Coca-Cola® doesn't just sell soda; it sells happiness. Nike® doesn't just sell shoes; it sells inspiration and empowerment. These brands know their USP and have built their empires around it.

Your DVP goes deeper. It's the part of you that keeps people engaged after the USP makes them look your way.

Companies use various scales to measure their value propositions. Each industry has standards, and most successful companies understand the need for a set of core values to propel them forward in their field.

In the dating world, there's no such universally agreed-upon system for evaluating a person's larger personal values. Believe it or not, you actually begin to create your own definition when you accept or reject a suggestion on a dating app. But this decision is usually based entirely on physical appearance and a short bio. Relationships are far more complex than a profile picture and a paragraph. We need a deeper, more comprehensive way to evaluate and position ourselves in the dating landscape.

This is where the DVP concept comes in. To truly understand your own strengths, attract the right partner, and make informed decisions about potential matches, you need to position yourself with a well-articulated and unique value proposition.

The idea of a Dating Value Proposition emerged as I uncovered the fundamental question we need to ask when we're searching for a lifetime partner: **what key attributes do people use to make dating decisions?** Through extensive research, observation, and conversation, many discovered that early-stage romantic attraction is influenced by a combination of physical traits, personality, behavioral cues, mutual interest, and biological responses, which together drive the decision to pursue a potential partner.

The list of things people look for could have been expanded into twenty-five or more topics, but I knew we needed something simple. So, I drew upon another marketing concept—the MECE (Mutually Exclusive, Collectively Exhaustive). This system breaks concepts into distinct, non-overlapping categories that together cover everything. In other words, when we define something as MECE, we reveal everything that matters without redundancy.

When I started to drill down on the MECE of dating, I thought about the things that float to the top of the conversation when we discuss dating possibilities with our friends. Stop and think about what you would do if a good friend called and said, "Hey, I've got a co-worker I think you would really like. I think you two should go out." Do you blindly agree? Most people instinctively start filtering the hypothetical date by asking some basic questions.

- What do they look like?
- What do they do?
- What are they like?
- Are they smart? What are their interests?

These questions reflect the core attributes that shape the way we evaluate potential partners both consciously and subconsciously. Using the MECE Principle, we can narrow down our list of attractions to The Four Fundamental Pillars of Dating—Mind, Body, Soul, and Resources.

Using the Pillars, you can dig deeper to identify your personal DVP. When you understand your current strengths and recognize areas for growth, you're better able to present your authentic self in the best light. Positioning in marketing as well as dating asks, "What do you bring to the table?"

Each Pillar of our DVP has been formed by past experience. Fortunately, we have the power to grow and mold each one, but to discover our unique DVPs and determine the areas that need work, we have to evaluate the current state of our Pillars.

- **Mind**—This Pillar covers our intelligence, creativity, and problem-solving abilities. A sharp mind not only allows for engaging conversations but also contributes to shared decision-making and emotional understanding in a relationship. We have to remember not to limit intelligence to academic knowledge or education level. Intelligence is multi-faceted. It also includes street smarts and life skills.
- **Body**—Physical attractiveness is often the first impression others have of you. But it's not just about how you look. Your health, vitality, and overall lifestyle also fall under this category. Taking care of your body through fitness, grooming, and healthy habits enhances how others perceive you and how you feel about yourself.
- **Soul**—Your soul is the essence of your values, character, and emotional depth. This includes kindness, empathy, spiritual beliefs, and the ability to connect on a deeper level. Some call this emotional intelligence (EQ). A strong soul element often means navigating challenges with resilience and maintaining meaningful connections.
- **Resources**—This Pillar refers to what you can offer in terms of stability and support—financially. It's more than just how much money you make. It includes your lifestyle and career ambitions, as well as your ideas about spending and saving.

I have another acronym for you to remember: the Four Fundamental Pillars of Dating. For the ladies, it's "B. Mrs."

The gentlemen can remember that they are looking for "Mrs. B." You see, it doesn't matter which order you put them in. The true importance is in recognizing these four vital areas. Each person will have to rank the components for themselves. (Don't worry, I'll share a way to get that ranking later.)

## The Dating Value Proposition Compass

To help visualize DVP, I like to think of it as a compass. Just as a compass provides direction and helps with navigation, these four attributes give you a holistic understanding of yourself and others. And the four points on the DVP compass[IP] reflect the balance we strive for in our dating value proposition.

At the top of the compass, we put Soul. This represents God, spirituality, and the intangible qualities that make us who we are. Our emotional intelligence, values, and relational depth act like a magnetic north. We need a strong signal from this portion of our compass so we know which direction to move.

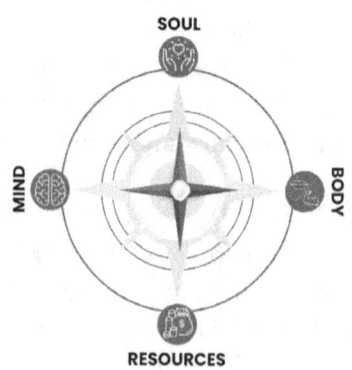

DATING VALUE PROPOSITION (DVP)

Resources fall at the bottom of our compass, representing the tangible, grounded aspects of life—income, stability, and the ability to provide or contribute to a shared life. These provide a secure foundation. Much like a magnet, we often feel this north-south polarity pushing, pulling, and causing friction.

Those who focus intensely on the soul often detach from material concerns. I think of spiritual leaders like monks and other deeply philosophical individuals who have decided to forsake wealth in favor of enlightenment, ethical living, or an unwavering commitment to a higher purpose.

Conversely, those who accumulate immense resources sometimes find themselves less concerned with their soul. Financial security means they don't worry about mortality like they might have before. Life becomes easier, and many ethical questions become irrelevant when wealth can solve their problems. A billionaire, for instance, may not be concerned about fairness or charity because their needs are always met.

Neither extreme is inherently good or bad. But the best case is a balance between soul and resources. When we find that sweet spot in the middle, we recognize that though financial power provides security and comfort, a strong soul offers depth, purpose, and true fulfillment.

A similar tug-of-war goes on between the right and left sides of the compass. On the right, we find body—the active, visible aspects of physical attractiveness and health. On the left, there's mind, the intellectual and often less visible aspects of our curiosity, knowledge, and mental agility.

The current stereotype suggests that athletes, models, or those focused on beauty neglect intellectual pursuits. The "jock" and "cheerleader" archetypes reflect a world where physical attractiveness or strength can sometimes provide opportunities that intellect otherwise would.

Conversely, the scholars, scientists, and intellectuals often place less emphasis on their physical form. The "nerd" stereotype exists because intelligence can open doors, reducing the need for external validation through appearance.

Yet, true power comes when these two are in harmony. A person who sharpens both Mind and Body creates an intelligent and commanding presence. They navigate the world with strategic thinking and physical confidence.

Understanding your DVP allows you to recognize where you land on the compass and where tensions exist. Many people gravitate toward certain elements while neglecting others. Without proper balance, you'll create a label for yourself.

- **The Thinker** (Strong Mind, Weak Body)— Prioritizes intelligence but may struggle with physical presence or health.
- **The Athlete** (Strong Body, Weak Mind)— Dominates in physical realms but may lack deeper intellectual pursuits.
- **The Spiritualist** (Strong Soul, Weak Resources)— Deeply moral and connected but struggles with financial success.
- **The Capitalist** (Strong Resources, Weak Soul)— Wealthy and successful but lacks depth and meaning.

In order to Date Like a Brand, you'll need to develop all four elements. Even if one dominates, you don't want it to do so at the expense of the others. A person who nurtures Mind, Body, Soul, and Resources equally becomes unstoppable—capable of achieving greatness while remaining deeply connected to their values and purpose. The DVP Compass is not about choosing one element over another; it is about learning how to navigate the forces that shape our lives so we can move forward with clarity, power, and balance.

Additionally, understanding your DVP allows you to navigate the dating marketplace strategically. Just as a brand must evaluate itself against competitors to attract the right customers, you need to assess your strengths and honestly compare them to others in the dating pool. We don't want to create competition or start to feel bad about ourselves. This assessment is in no way negative. It's about clarity. It allows you to:

- **Present Yourself Authentically**—When you recognize your strengths, you can honestly acknowledge what you bring to the table.
- **Recognize Compatibility**—The Four Fundamental Pillars of Dating allow you to more readily understand what you're looking for in a partner and identify those who align with your values and goals.
- **Focus on Growth**—The clarity these Pillars bring will help you see where growth could make you your best self and a stronger partner.

This Mind, Body, Soul, Resources Quadrilateral allows you to shift your mindset from superficial, one-dimensional app swiping to meaningful evaluation and connection.

## Understanding the Bell Curve

Before evaluating ourselves, we must develop a scale for each category. Brands assess their strengths and weaknesses with a quantitative rating. A numeric scale helps them track their progress and see their growth or movement over time. It also gives them a way to view themselves objectively compared to their competition.

As a brand, you need to develop a similar quantitative understanding. Self-awareness is key to understanding what you offer in a relationship. But to simplify this, the dating world needs a calibrated equal-playing-field approach to this assessment. In order to get accurate results, we have to be as objective as possible with the inputs, and we need to understand where we fall on the bell curve.

A common myth accompanies ratings and rankings. Many believe if you rate something on a scale of one to ten, each number represents 10 percent of the population. For example, they assume in a group of ten people, one person will rank "1," one will rank "10," and the rest will neatly fill in the numbers in between. The chart for such a group would look something like this chart you see. But that's not how the world works, and it's certainly not how we find traits distributed among people.

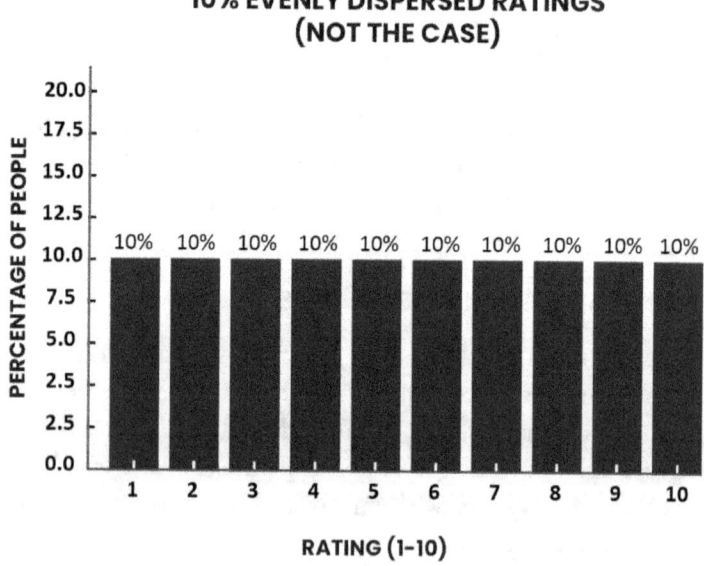

The truth is, most people cluster around the middle of the scale, with fewer individuals at the extreme ends. This natural distribution forms what statisticians call a Gaussian Curve. You've probably heard it referred to as a bell curve or normal distribution. Named for its distinctive shape, the bell curve is a statistical model used to represent the way traits, behaviors, or characteristics are distributed across a population. The curve is widest in the middle, where the majority of people fall, and tapers off at either end, representing the smaller number of individuals with extreme values.

Whether we're measuring physical attractiveness, intelligence, or financial resources, most people fall within a range close to the average, while only a small percentage truly embody the "exceptional" or "subpar" extremes.

## A "NORMAL" BELL CURVE

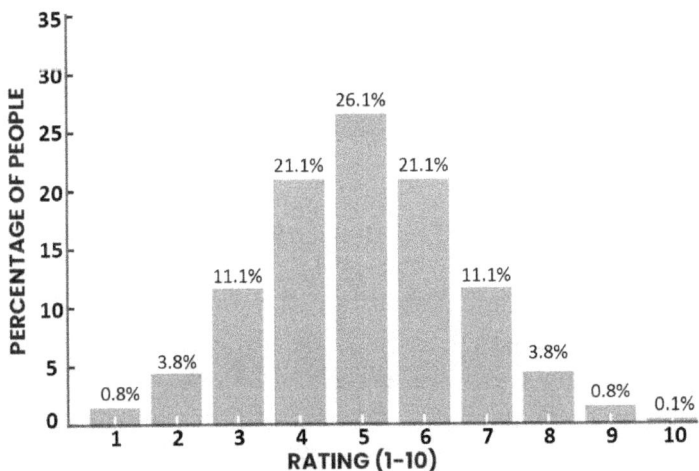

This same principle applies to other traits like weight, or in the dating world, the parts of your DVP—physical attractiveness, financial resources, intelligence, and your soul.

Consider height. Most men in the United States reach about 5'9". Still, we know some NBA players measure 6'5" or taller, and racehorse owners look for jockeys who are 5'2" or shorter. We also recognize that these extreme ends of the spectrum are naturally rare.

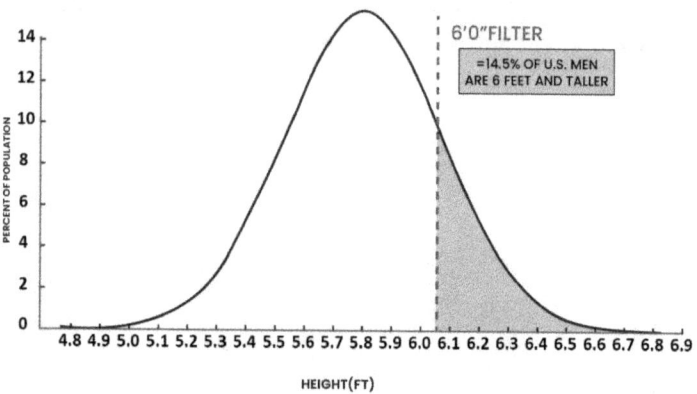

Understanding this concept is critical when evaluating yourself in the dating marketplace. If you've ever looked around and thought, "Where are all the tens?" the answer is simple: there aren't many. Similarly, if you feel like a three or four in certain areas, you're likely not alone—because most people aren't extreme outliers either. In the dating pool, the middle isn't something to dread. Most people are doing just fine there.

In the context of dating, understanding the bell curve takes you into the market with realism and self-awareness. It reminds us that being stable, sincere, and lovable are tremendous traits. Many people overestimate their own position or underestimate others, leading to mismatched expectations. The bell curve reminds us we don't have to feel like we fall short if we're not all a ten. When we recognize that most people fall into the middle—neither "perfect" nor "unattractive," neither "wealthy" nor "poor"—it can help recalibrate our perspective and expectations. If you're a five or six, congratulations, you're right in the sweet spot of the dating market.

When we consider the four aspects of our compass, the bell curve gives us clarity.

- **Intelligence:** Though the DVP takes more than mere IQ into account, the truth is, on a scale of 6 to 200, 50 percent of the population falls within the 91-110 IQ level. Only 15 or 16 percent land in the 10 points above and below that average, and less than 1 percent hit 140 or above—the genius range. That middle section of the graph curves like a beautiful bell.
- **Physical Attractiveness:** The idea that 10 percent of the population scores a ten and 10 percent get a one is simply not true. The vast majority of people cluster in the middle of the attractiveness scale, with a smaller number at either end.
- **Emotional Intelligence:** While some individuals are exceptionally empathetic or self-aware, most people exhibit average levels of emotional intelligence, with only a few outliers on either side.
- **Financial Resources:** Similarly, only a small percentage of people have extraordinary wealth or struggle with extreme poverty. The bell curve would be quite high at the $50,000 annual salary range because about half the population falls in this category. Most individuals fall into a middle-income range that supports a comfortable, if not extravagant, lifestyle.

By accepting that most people live in the middle of the curve, you can start to view yourself and others more objectively. This isn't about lowering standards; it's about grounding your standards in reality. If you insist on finding someone who is exceptional in every category, you may be searching for a statistical anomaly. Similarly, if you feel inadequate because you don't rank at the extreme end of a trait, you're forgetting that most people are right there with you between three and seven in the center of the curve.

When evaluating your DVP—your Mind, Body, Soul, and Resources—it's essential to assess where you truly fall within the spectrum of traits. Are you a top performer in one area? Perhaps you're closer to average in another. Recognizing this can empower you as you identify your strengths, address opportunities for growth, and avoid chasing unrealistic dreams.

This approach is not about putting yourself down; it's about embracing reality to make better choices. By understanding the bell curve, you can:

- Focus on areas where you naturally excel.
- Recognize and appreciate the strengths in others.
- Avoid unrealistic comparisons or expectations.

In the dating world, the bell curve reminds us that everyone brings a mix of strengths and challenges to the table. Just as brands differentiate themselves in a crowded marketplace, you don't need to be perfect in every area. Instead, you need to highlight your unique DVP and attract someone who values it.

## Take Action

Now that you have crafted a USP, consider how you can best communicate it in your online profiles, conversations, and

## Positioning

actions. Your USP and DVP must be more than something you tell people; they should be evident in your actions.

_____

_____

_____

When you understand your Mind, Body, Soul, and Resources, dating transforms from a random process to a strategic one. The DVP becomes a foundation for dating success. It empowers you to:

- ✓ Know what strengths you bring to the table
- ✓ Identify what truly matters in a partner
- ✓ Avoid superficial selection mistakes
- ✓ Date with clarity, confidence, and strategy

I want you to start exploring your DVP action steps, but first, we need to dive a bit deeper into each one. So, before we move to Step Four, I will help you assess where you are in each of these Pillars.

It's important to remember that Dating like a Brand isn't about lying to yourself. It's about knowing exactly where you stand and then marketing yourself strategically into better and better markets.

Remember, your DVP is unique to you. We aren't striving for perfection in every area. We assess so we can embrace our strengths, look at our opportunities honestly, and find someone who values what we bring to the table. It's time to prepare for the final three parts of the Platform by identifying your brand.

# CHAPTER SEVEN

# Assessing the Mind

*An investment in knowledge pays the best interest.*
—Benjamin Franklin

*The beautiful thing about learning is nobody can take it away from you.*
—B.B. King

The mind is an essential component of your DVP. It encompasses intelligence, curiosity, creativity, and the ability to navigate both intellectual and emotional challenges. A strong mind allows for meaningful conversations, effective problem-solving, and emotional understanding—key elements for building and sustaining a relationship.

Most people have heard of the two main kinds of intelligence. Those who graduate at the top of their class possess **Academic Intelligence**—some call it book smarts. **Practical Intelligence**, also known as street smarts, helps people cope with the trials of life with a bit more ease.

To look at it with an even broader lens, Howard Gardner argued there are nine different kinds of intelligence, some that fall in the category of academic intelligence and others that would be considered street smarts: Linguistic, Mathematical, Spatial, Bodily, Musical, Interpersonal, Intrapersonal, Naturalist, and Existential.[4] None are superior to the others, but understanding them and where they rank in importance to you can help you provide actionable steps to enhance your mental value.

## Understanding the Two Components of the Mind

Academic intelligence refers to your ability to learn, reason, and solve problems. We measure it through traditional metrics like IQ, education level, and cognitive skills. Market perception often puts more weight on education level than on the other indicators of academic intelligence. Letters behind a name give people a little more attention; however, it's important to remember this is market perception rather than your innate worth. At the same time, with or without a degree, this form of intelligence is often attractive because it signals capability, ambition, and resourcefulness. High academic intelligence brings significant advantages:

- Strong analytical and logical reasoning skills.
- Ability to engage in thought-provoking conversations.
- Curiosity and a willingness to learn.

Practical Intelligence, or street smarts, refers to the ability to navigate real-world situations effectively. It includes common sense and adaptability. While academic intelligence helps with theoretical problem-solving, practical intelligence focuses on useful applications and social dynamics. This kind of brain power is helpful in many situations:

- Quick thinking in unexpected situations.
- Strong interpersonal skills and emotional awareness.
- Ability to read social cues and adapt to different environments.

Whether you put more weight on the practical or academic mind, don't forget to look for other important aspects like a sense of humor and social awareness. While you might picture Sheldon from *The Big Bang Theory* when you imagine a high IQ, it's important to note that a good sense of humor is also a sign of a great mind. It takes highly developed observational skills and a quick wit to craft a layered joke or see humor in the details of the moment.

Some of the best comedians aren't just funny; they're brilliant. It takes cognitive ability to play with language, leverage timing, and keep everything in a social context. A great sense of humor is more than just charming; it's a mark of a sharp, highly adaptive mind. Sometimes the people who make you laugh the hardest are also the smartest.

Like the common evaluation system used in social groups for appearance, we can put the mind on a rating scale. As we mentioned, we can measure intelligence on a bell curve, so most people fall into the four to six range for mental value. Regardless of the type of intelligence that's most valuable to you, this rating scale can help you determine your own Mental Value Proposition:

| Rating | Description |
|--------|-------------|
| 10 | Genius-level intellect with exceptional emotional and social intelligence. Regularly contributes at the highest levels of thought, innovation, or public influence. Likely holds an advanced degree (e.g., PhD, MD, JD) or equivalent distinction through invention, authorship, or national/global recognition. Their thinking not only solves problems—it shapes people and systems. |
| 9 | Brilliant across academic and/or practical domains. Often holds a graduate degree or equivalent credential and is known within their industry or community as a thought leader, expert, or advisor. They regularly mentor others, lead discussions, or publish ideas. Clear evidence of structured, high-level thinking. |
| 8 | Exceptionally sharp in academic, technical, or practical intelligence. Likely completed college or has pursued advanced training in their field. Stands out among peers for their problem-solving, insight, or strategic thinking. May be known locally or professionally for good judgment, persuasive communication, or innovative ideas. |

| Rating | Description |
|---|---|
| 7 | Highly intelligent and mentally agile. College education is common at this level, though strong vocational or entrepreneurial performance can substitute. Demonstrates clear-headedness, curiosity, and the ability to analyze or synthesize across various domains. Often has leadership potential and shows a deep understanding of people and ideas. |
| 6 | Above-average intelligence or strong street smarts. May or may not have completed college but demonstrates keen reasoning, emotional fluency, and good instincts. Typically excels in real-world problem-solving and practical domains. Formal education may be limited, but awareness and clarity are present. |
| 5 | Functional and average in both academic and applied thinking. Likely completed high school and possibly some college or training. Capable of managing life's routine challenges but not particularly intellectually curious or strategic. Reliable and steady but not mentally distinctive. |
| 4 | Slightly below average in processing, analysis, or adaptability. May not have completed high school or had limited exposure to rigorous academic thinking. Tends to avoid complexity and may rely heavily on habit or intuition. Can function well in structured settings but struggles when context shifts. |

| Rating | Description |
|---|---|
| 3 | Limited practical or academic intelligence. Often misinterprets nuance, misses context, or struggles to adapt to unexpected problems. Communication may feel disjointed or overly literal. Unlikely to have completed high school, though some basic functional knowledge is present. |
| 2 | Below-average reasoning or awareness. Has difficulty with abstract thinking or navigating new environments. Often needs support or direction to interpret situations. May lack formal education and emotional self-awareness. |
| 1 | Significant cognitive or emotional limitations. Unable to function independently in problem-solving, communication, or relational awareness. Reasoning is severely impaired; often reliant on others for guidance or understanding. |

Fortunately, if you feel like your mental value rating is lower than it should be, there are things you can do to improve it. Few will ever reach nine or ten, but moving from a three to a six or seven to eight is possible. There are three areas of potential growth in the realm of the mind: academic intelligence, practical intelligence, and communication skills.

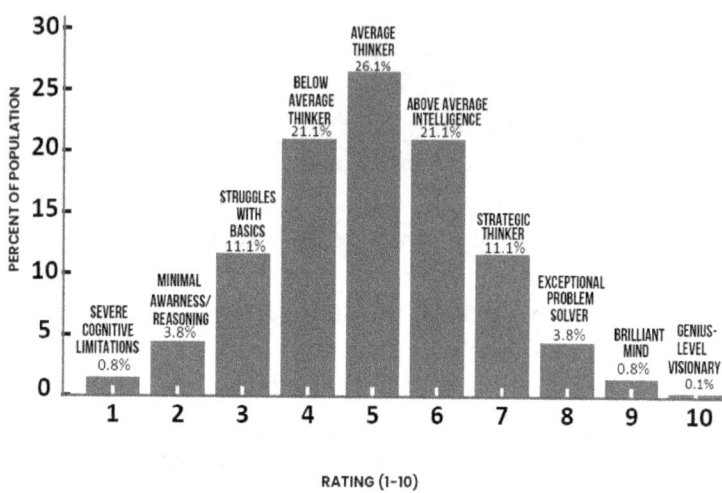

## Expanding Your Mental Value

Curiosity will be your greatest tool in enhancing your academic intelligence. Regardless of your interests, you'll find books, websites, and podcasts to expand your knowledge in those arenas. By exploring topics you hadn't considered before, you might stumble upon information that intrigues you and draws you in. Developing a curious nature opens the doors to all kinds of things you didn't know interested you. Even hobbies can increase your academic intelligence. Push yourself to get better at what you enjoy, or try new endeavors to ignite new neurotransmitters in your brain. Find puzzles or games that challenge you, learn new skills, or embark on a new language journey.

Practical Intelligence often comes from the school of hard knocks. This means we may need to step out of our comfort zone and take on real-world problems more often.

## Assessing the Mind

Budgeting, planning trips, and organizing events can help you develop the quick thinking that comes with street smarts as well as resiliency and the ability to adapt to unplanned situations.

Communication Skills rank high when you consider things that can help build or break a relationship. It's vital to learn to articulate your thoughts clearly and confidently. Start with a trusted friend. Practice active conversations that begin with high-level topics, such as what you are learning as you increase your academic intelligence. Find topics that challenge and engage your partner.

Some people excel in academic intelligence, while others thrive in practical intelligence. Trying to achieve ultra-high levels in both areas will simply frustrate you, but everyone can develop a balance that enhances their overall mental value. Using the ten-point scale above can help you recognize your strengths and identify areas for growth. And it can also help you recognize people whose mental attributes complement your own.

While you might not want a partner whose mind scale is your clone, you do want someone who aligns with your intellectual and practical needs. For example, if you value stimulating conversations, you'll want to look for someone who enjoys learning and debating. If you love thinking on your feet or lack basic street smarts, you should prioritize a partner with strong, practical problem-solving skills.

A strong mental connection fosters understanding, collaboration, and resilience in a relationship. This can easily be a cornerstone for long-term relationship success.

## Take Action

Being honest with yourself will give you tremendous self-awareness as you assess your DVP in the Four Foundational Pillars of Dating. Consider these questions before you move on:

1. Where do you fall on the Bell Curve of Academic Intelligence?

   _____
   _____

2. What ranking would you give yourself for Practical Intelligence?

   _____
   _____

3. How would you rank your Communication Skills?

   _____
   _____

4. Would you like to increase any of those scores?

   _____
   _____

5. Which one(s)? _____

6. If yes, what are your next steps to reach your goal?

   _____
   _____
   _____

7. Which of these three is most important to you as you look toward Partnership Performance?

    a. Academic Intelligence
    b. Practical Intelligence
    c. Communication Skills

8. According to the descriptions above, where do you fall on the Mind Bell Curve?

    _____
    _____

# CHAPTER EIGHT

# Assessing the Body

*Beauty is about enhancing what you have. Let yourself shine through!*
—Janelle Monáe

*Beauty is in the eye of the beholder.*
—Margaret Wolfe Hungerford

The way we look often becomes the first impression we make on others. It acts as an initial filter in the dating process. Physical appearance catches people's attention before other qualities like intelligence, kindness, or compatibility.

## The Two Main Ways to Assess the Body

The body Pillar of our four-focus foundation has two primary components—**Physical Attractiveness** and **Genetic Fitness**.

Cultural standards, media influence, and evolutionary psychology shape the current standards for physical attractiveness. For instance, between 1500 and 1800, a person who carried extra weight was considered more beautiful. Thin people wore bulky garments to perpetuate the illusion.[5] While beauty is subjective, nearly every culture and time period has recognized certain traits as attractive due to their links to health and vitality. These include symmetrical features, clear skin, good posture, and physical fitness.

Additionally, cleanliness, neatness, and personal hygiene significantly impact how others perceive you. A healthy body reflects self-care and discipline. Clothing, accessories, and overall presentation will enhance or detract from physical appeal.

Genetic fitness refers to the biological qualities that signal reproductive health and vitality. Evolutionary psychology suggests that people unconsciously seek partners whose traits indicate strong genes for future offspring. Many traits that add to an appealing physical appearance are indicators of high survival and reproduction rates. For instance, clear skin indicates good health and absence of disease, facial symmetry suggests genetic stability and developmental health, and high energy levels reflect physical health and vitality.

Nearly everyone has at least heard someone rate someone of the opposite sex on a scale of one to ten. Unfortunately, the traditional continuum is left open to personal perceptions. So I've created a more structured way to factor how the opposite sex reacts to you. This more standardized scale can help you self-assess more objectively.

## The Body Bell Curve

As with every area we will assess, the body runs on a bell curve, with most people falling between three and seven. And as much as we hate to think about it, five will be the average and most prevalent.

| Rating | Description |
|--------|-------------|
| 10 | **Exceptional Looking: Model-Level Beauty**<br>• Universally stunning; impossible to ignore.<br>• Regularly approached or harassed in public by strangers.<br>• Likely to have modeling or entertainment opportunities.<br>• People often comment on their appearance without prompting.<br>• They receive constant validation from both sexes, often to an overwhelming degree. |
| 9 | **Near Perfection: Strikingly Attractive**<br>• Extremely attractive, with only minor imperfections.<br>• People stare or glance frequently, and strangers may still approach.<br>• Frequently receives compliments on their looks.<br>• Attracts significant attention in social settings, but they come across as slightly more relatable than a 10. |

| Rating | Description |
|---|---|
| 8 | **Very Attractive: The "Head Turner"**<br>• Regularly considered attractive by most people they encounter.<br>• Receives compliments and positive attention, though less often than a 9 or 10.<br>• Often noticed in a group but may not be universally overwhelming in appearance.<br>• A strong, polished presentation can elevate them closer to a 9. |
| 7 | **Attractive: Above Average**<br>• Consistently appealing to many but not striking.<br>• Likely to be noticed in social settings, though not the center of attention.<br>• Receives compliments, but it might depend more on their style, grooming, or charisma.<br>• Often called "cute," "handsome," or "pretty." |

| Rating | Description |
|---|---|
| 6 | **Slightly Above Average: Pleasant to Look At**<br>• Appealing and likable, though not overwhelmingly attractive.<br>• Attracts attention with effort (e.g., styling, fitness, or grooming).<br>• Most of their attractiveness is perceived as natural but enhanced by presentation.<br>• Rarely outshines others in a group setting, but they can stand out with confidence or charm. |
| 5 | **Average: The Baseline**<br>• Neither particularly attractive nor unattractive; this person blends in. Represents the average perception of physical appearance in the population.<br>• People rarely comment specifically on their looks, positively or negatively.<br>• Attractiveness might improve significantly with effort in areas like fitness, style, or grooming. |

| Rating | Description |
|---|---|
| 4 | **Slightly Below Average**<br>• Some noticeable features that might not fit conventional standards of beauty.<br>• Rarely complimented on looks unless they make an extra effort.<br>• Can improve perceptions with better grooming, fitness, or style.<br>• May not be the first choice in a group but can attract attention through personality or charm. |
| 3 | **Below Average: Noticeable Flaws**<br>• Physical attributes might limit their perceived attractiveness.<br>• Rarely receive unsolicited attention for their looks.<br>• May have features that are culturally or socially less favored.<br>• People might overlook them at first but can be won over by other traits. |

| Rating | Description |
|---|---|
| 2 | **Unconventional Appearance**<br>• Significant deviations from societal beauty norms.<br>• Rarely, if ever, receive compliments on their appearance.<br>• Struggles to attract attention based on looks alone.<br>• Often need to rely on personality, intellect, or other attributes to make a connection. |
| 1 | **Severe Physical Deformities or Extreme Outliers**<br>• Noticeable, significant physical differences that negatively draw attention.<br>• Rarely perceived as attractive in a conventional sense.<br>• Often experience visible judgment or discomfort from others.<br>• Personality and other traits become the primary focus for building connections. |

Unlike the assessment of the mind, the body rating focuses more on perception. Your ranking is based on how others react, not personal self-esteem. So to assess our physical attractiveness, we have to reflect on objective signs of how we are treated regarding our looks. Do you receive compliments or stares? Do you find yourself ignored? This Physical

Appearance scale means we must set aside our biases and be honest about how others respond to us.

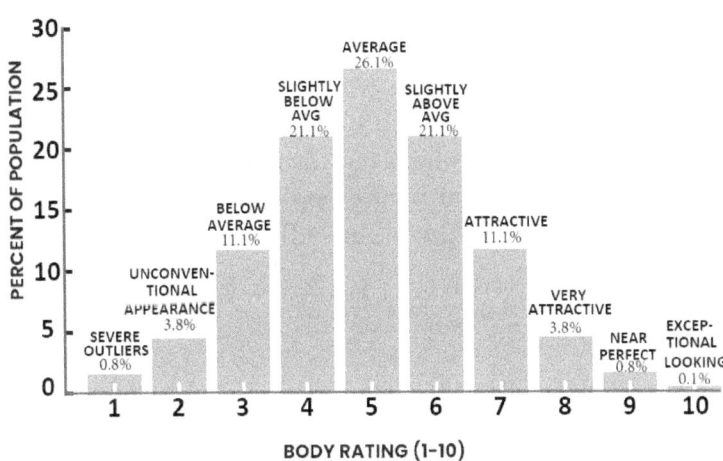

Because the Body and Attractiveness Bell Curve is so subjective, I put the mean at 5 in my graphic. As I mentioned, beauty standards vary significantly across regions and time periods. Social media, television, movies, and advertising create unrealistic beauty expectations, leading many to chase unattainable ideals.

However, understanding these influences can help you focus on genuine self-improvement rather than societal pressures. And understanding that being a five or six actually puts you in the most prevalent range can help you overcome insecurities.

## The Difficult Truth

One of the disaster points in marketing is mispriced products. Set the price too high, and the market will leave you behind. Set the price too low, and you'll undervalue yourself and attract the wrong buyers. Dating is no different.

And while it's common to over- or underestimate your rating for any of the four pillars, when it comes to the Body Pillar, everyone thinks they're a seven. And even worse, most people believe they deserve at least a seven in a partner. But if we want success in dating, we have to look for truth rather than fleeting hopes and wishful thinking.

When it comes to physical attraction, we need to be realistic. About 68 percent of the population falls within one standard deviation of the mean—effectively between a four and six out of ten.

I'm sorry, but very few are true sevens, eights, nines, or tens.

Fortunately, just as few are true ones, twos, or threes.

Only about 13.6 percent of people fall in the seven range. And an eight or higher? Only about 2.1 percent. Are you looking for a nine or a ten? Your odds are fractional—maybe 0.1–0.5 percent.[6]

Statistically speaking, if everyone thinks they're a seven and everyone wants a seven or better, we have a massive marketplace mismatch.

One famous study asked college students to rate themselves on a scale of one to ten for attractiveness and set the minimum level of attractiveness they would accept in a dating partner. Over 30 percent rated themselves a seven or higher, and almost everyone said they would only date someone seven or above. It's statistically impossible.[7]

It's like walking into a car dealership where every buyer says they deserve a Ferrari, but 87 percent have a Honda budget.

## Assessing the Body

In marketing, when a brand overestimates its own value, it leads to:

- Disappointment (buyers don't respond)
- Frustration (the brand blames the buyers)
- Stagnation (the brand never adapts)
- Collapse (the brand dies off in the market)

In dating, if you rate yourself inaccurately, you may set standards that leave you single indefinitely. You also have the potential to miss out on all the wonderful people who match your true brand. A rating that doesn't align with the truth will cause you to experience endless frustration. You'll end up feeling like there are no good options when, in reality, the mismatch is in the mirror.

Wanting a seven or more doesn't make you a seven.

Thinking you're a seven or more doesn't make you a seven or eight.

The chart reveals one of the biggest mismatches in modern dating. Nearly half the population falls in the range of 5 to 6.9. Unfortunately, many of these average-looking people seek partners in the 7 to 9 range. With only 15.9 percent of the population there, we can see the "math ain't mathin'." A 2010 study by Cooper and others backs this up. Most participants in their survey rated themselves a seven, yet said they were looking for a seven or higher. Men and women alike set these high standards; however, men were less likely to deviate.[8]

## DATING MATH DILEMMA: THE SCARCITY OF 7'S AND ABOVE

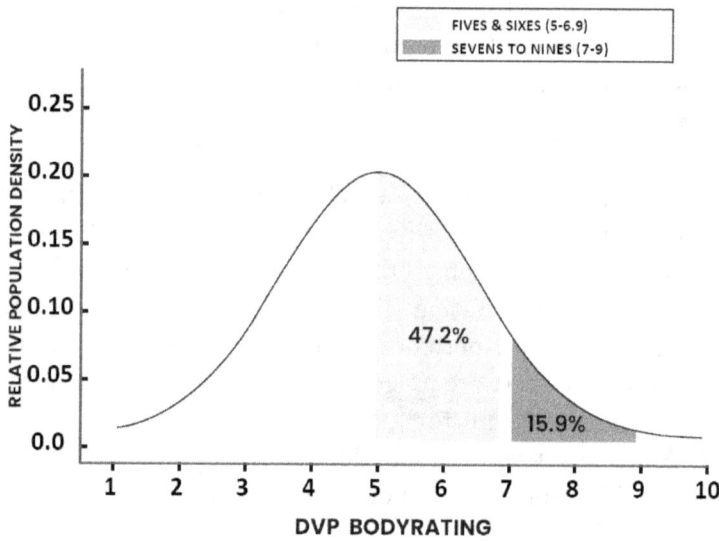

This creates a demand glut in the upper end of the dating pool. It looks a lot like mid-tier brands trying to compete for the high-end shelf space without significant upgrades. When expectations rise faster than value, frustration is inevitable.

Your DVP, especially when it comes to your Body pillar, must be assessed honestly, not aspirationally. To calibrate your actual rating, evaluate the market feedback and analyze the data.

Are the people choosing you the kind of people you want, or do you feel like you have to put excessive work in to attract the sevens?

Ask three honest friends to anonymously rate your looks, or watch how your profile picture performs on apps with a wide reach.

ASSESSING THE BODY

If you're getting average attention from average markets, you're likely in the four to six zone. You can potentially increase your score by one if you maximize your presentation; however, if you're already working hard in the areas of fitness, grooming, and health, you might just be kidding yourself.

When you have a reality-calibrated view of yourself, you waste less time chasing mismatches. You can also focus your energy on realistic, high-quality connections, and by improving incrementally over time, you can boost your DVP naturally.

Honesty is your greatest strength as you evaluate your position because the truth is, most people are not a seven. But if you think about it, that's not depressing, it's empowering. It means with real work, you can outshine others in your category and become the best version of yourself in reality, not fantasy.

## Improving Your Body Value

While genetics plays a significant role in physical appearance, factors such as smoking, a poor diet, lack of exercise, and neglecting grooming can lower your attractiveness score. On the other hand, regular workouts, healthy eating, good sleep habits, and polished grooming enhance attractiveness. Even confidence levels and the way a person presents themselves can make a difference. Your lifestyle choices have the power to shift your rating two points down or one point up.

The 2006 movie *The Devil Wears Prada* painted a vivid picture of how someone can transform from a six to an eight or nine. The journalist morphed from a woman with no fashion sense, frizzy hair, unattractive glasses, and tremendous insecurity to someone who was trendy, classy, and confident. And more than one movie mountain man has turned from a big, hairy, scary five into a ruggedly handsome clean-cut seven.

The first step in assessing your current rating is to be honest but kind to yourself. Use the scale and bell curve to gauge your current position, then set realistic goals to ensure you can be your best possible self.

Adopting a healthy lifestyle can enhance your overall health to raise your rating by a point or two. A more balanced diet affects skin tone and aging as well as weight and potential muscle. Adequate sleep not only reduces the chances of long-term health effects; it also improves skin color and the beauty of the eyes.

Don't be afraid to invest in yourself in any of these areas, and remember to celebrate your strengths. Highlight the features you're proud of and learn to carry yourself with confidence. Remember, brands optimize their packaging, messaging, and visibility. And YOU can do the same.

Physical attractiveness matters, but it's only one component of a lasting relationship. While improving your body's value can boost your confidence and appeal, too often, it's given an inflated priority in the dating world. Other areas like mind, soul, and resources will provide you with a relationship of depth and resilience—attributes you'll need to endure life's challenges.

## Take Action

While you can't change your genetics, you can control your grooming and the daily habits that affect health-related factors. But before you begin, you need to determine your starting point.

1. Where would you rank yourself on the Body Bell Curve?

_____

_____

## Assessing the Body

2. Do you want that number to be higher?
   _____
   _____

3. If yes, what area(s) needs improvement?

   - Grooming/Hygiene
   - Style
   - Physique
   - General Health
   - Other: _____

4. Grooming and hygiene changes can happen overnight. Style might require a good friend or a professional stylist. Which of the following will you implement in the next ten days to reach your goals?

   - Visit a hair salon
   - Up my game with my grooming and hygiene
   - Hire a stylist or enlist the aid of a stylish friend
   - Go to the gym (or workout) at least _____ days a week
   - Hire a personal trainer
   - Enlist the aid of a nutritionist
   - _____

5. After you choose one or more to begin in ten days, select another to start within thirty days if necessary.
   _____
   _____

# CHAPTER NINE

# Assessing Your Resources

> *Money can't buy happiness,*
> *but it's a lot more comfortable to cry*
> *in a Mercedes than on a bicycle.*
> —Unknown

> *I'm not a businessman,*
> *I'm a business, man.*
> —Jay-Z

Some people feel shallow when they begin focusing on resources associated with relationships. But when we start to look for someone to build a life with, we have to be practical. That means resources turn into a key component of your Dating Value Proposition. Even those who put finances and assets into the minor consideration category must face the fact that twenty to forty percent of all marriages fail when they lack the stability and security resources provide, or when both people aren't on the same page.[9]

Disagreements over financial assets, the management of those assets, and the time and energy each person dedicates to increasing resources can sever relationships that are strong in the three other positions. Understanding the role resources play in measuring lifestyle compatibility is vital when you begin to look for a long-term partner.

## The Two Tiers of Resources

Like each of our other Pillars, resources have two layers—the **Current Financial Picture** and **Stability of Resources**.

Your financial picture—income, inherited wealth, family financial support, investments, and overall assets—creates the first tier in a secure and comfortable lifestyle. Each person will view the importance of these assets in vastly different ways. Some look for great wealth. They want to take a lot of vacations and drive the best cars. Others want enough to be comfortable but emphasize the soul or mind components more. The third option, a complete lack of resources, will strain any relationship.

On the other hand, resources are more than merely what a person owns. Stability, the second tier, might be even more critical. A consistent income, dependable job or growing business, and a strong work ethic can more than make up the difference in the wealth gap. Additionally, some of the wealth we mentioned, such as family trusts, inheritances, real estate, and other equity, can contribute to the stability of resources.

We also have to take into account how well we manage our assets. Wealth is not enough if you have reckless spending habits or poor financial planning. Stability means resources are used responsibly and consistently. When we add debt and the ability to save and invest, we begin to have a well-rounded idea of what long-term success looks like on the resources front.

## The Reality Check of the Resources Bell Curve

Many people assume that if you rate resources on a 1-to-10 scale, each rating will represent 10 percent of the population. Like the other Pillars, it just doesn't work that way. The Resources Bell Curve shows us that most people cluster around the middle—people with a little more or less than $150,000 in net worth and a salary of $60,000 a year. At the extreme ends, we see less than five percent of the population living in financial insecurity or being multimillionaires. Realistically, if your score is between a four and a seven, you're doing as well as most of the population, and truthfully, you can have a phenomenal life in that realm.

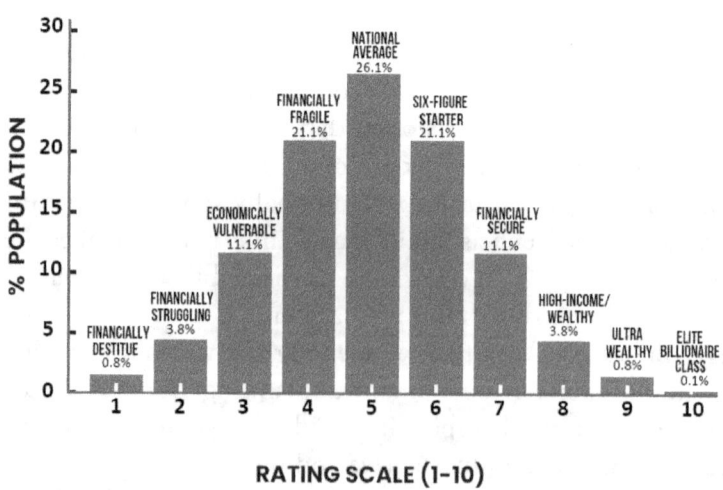

When we start to consider resources, it's important to note that money does not make the world go round. Your

## Assessing Your Resources

checkbook balance or net worth is insignificant when compared to what that money can help you do. Sadly, finances dictate where we live, the extras we can enjoy, and the schools our children can attend. The chart may be controversial and debatable because the exact numbers on net worth and income rely heavily on your location and lifestyle.

As you consider where you are on the scale, be aware that the biggest driver for this segmentation is not the money but the options money affords you, even if you choose not to take advantage of them. Understanding your own preferences and needs will help you determine your spot on the scale.

Let's look at the description of the Bell Curve Ratings for Resources:

| Rating | Description |
|---|---|
| 10 | **Billionaire-level wealth—Net Worth: $100 million and above** <br><br> Unparalleled financial freedom and access. Owns yachts, multiple luxury homes, private staff, or even islands. Regularly featured in major media or philanthropy circuits. Wealth is generational or tied to massive enterprise equity. Unparalleled financial freedom and access. |
| 9 | **Ultra Wealthy—Net Worth: $20 million–$99 million** <br><br> Likely owns multiple homes, invests heavily, and has elite financial advisors. Can fund entire ventures, foundations, or legacies. Still relatable to the wealthy class, but increasingly rarefied air. A+ celebs and superstar athletes. |

| Rating | Description |
|---|---|
| 8 | **High-Income / Wealthy—Net Worth: $5 million–$19 million; Annual Income: $750,000+**<br><br>Financially independent, even if still actively working. May own a second home, travel first-class, or invest in luxury assets. Can make lifestyle decisions with high autonomy. Often found among senior executives, law firm partners, or entrepreneurs. Working-level celebs and professional athletes. |
| 7 | **Financially Secure—Annual Income: $250,000–$749,000**<br><br>Provides a comfortable, low-stress lifestyle. Owns a well-maintained home, saves consistently, and invests wisely. Likely to afford elite private education, regular travel, and early retirement planning. Represents top earners in dual-income urban households or successful professionals. |
| 6 | **Six-Figure Starter—Annual Income: $100,000–$249,000**<br><br>Enters the respected "six-figure" tier. Can afford modest homeownership, a reliable car, and consistent savings. May have student loans or a young family. Represents high-achieving professionals, middle managers, or early-stage entrepreneurs with upside. |

## Assessing Your Resources

| Rating | Description |
|---|---|
| 5 | **National Average—Annual Income: ~$70,000**<br><br>Stable, self-sufficient, and typical of the working U.S. population. Able to manage bills, rent or mortgage, and occasional travel. May rely on budgeting to build wealth slowly. Represents the statistical midpoint for household income. |
| 4 | **Financially Frugal—Annual Income: $40,000–$69,000**<br><br>Can meet basic needs but often lives paycheck to paycheck. May lack health coverage or emergency savings. One unexpected bill can trigger financial instability. Often dependent on side jobs, roommates, or family support. |
| 3 | **Economically Vulnerable—Annual Income: $25,000–$39,000**<br><br>Struggles to maintain independence. Frequently behind on bills or rent. Few assets or savings. May rely on public programs or charitable support. Access to stable relationships may be constrained by economic stress. |
| 2 | **Financially Struggling—Annual Income: $10,000–$24,000**<br><br>Severely limited options. Faces regular food, housing, or utility insecurity. Cannot maintain a car or a stable residence without aid. Often in survival mode and focused on immediate needs. |

| Rating | Description |
|---|---|
| 1 | **Financially Destitute—Annual Income: <$10,000**<br><br>Little or no independent financial means. Dependent on others or the system for basic survival. Long-term relationship formation is impaired by overwhelming economic hardship. |

## Assessing Your Current Resources

Unlike the other three pillars, the category of Resources has a much less subjective rating. Either you can pay all your bills, save for future expenses, and prepare adequately for retirement, or you can't. Additionally, because most people begin dating long before they've reached their peak performance years, you have to take that into account when figuring resources.

Suppose you run into someone under thirty who doesn't have many assets. In that case, it's easier to gauge their future potential by evaluating their spending and saving habits, the way they maximize their talents, and their work ethic.

In marketing, we understand Resources are not static. They evolve based on effort, opportunities, and decisions. When we work to build a brand in the business world, we estimate the Net Present Value (NPV) of an asset. And despite how it sounds, this number is based on current as well as future numbers. The formula we use looks something like this:

NPV = Current Resources + Projected Future Resources (discounted for uncertainty)

## Assessing Your Resources

Each of the areas we use to determine someone's NPV also has the potential to be an area of growth for your own Resources Score.

1. List your current Resources indicators. Consider which ones you could use for growth, and use these as you evaluate your possible dates.

    a. **Education**: Pursuing a degree or certification might mean your paycheck isn't as big right now, but include the potential earnings upon completion in your NPV.
    b. **Career Path**: Are you in a field with high growth potential, or are you in a dead-end job? Careers in the technical fields, healthcare, finance, and the trades offer room to move up with significant pay increases.
    c. **Ambition and Drive**: Do you have clear goals and the motivation to achieve them, or are you simply coasting along?

2. Assess your lifestyle choices as well as the choices of partners.

    a. **Spending Habits**: Do you invest in your future, either through education or savings? Or do you blow your paycheck on luxuries above your means?
    b. **Risk Tolerance**: Are you reckless with money? Do you find yourself gambling or looking for get-rich-quick schemes? Or perhaps you're overly cautious—you wish you could hide your money under the mattress so no one could take it. A middle ground approach usually works best.

c. **Assess the Potential Partner:** You should heavily discount the NPV of a person with poor spending habits, an inability to save, or irresponsible or impulsive tendencies.

3. Factor in family wealth

   a. Do you have access to generational wealth or other financial safety nets?
   b. If so, are you a responsible steward of these funds?

4. Watch for the intangibles

   a. Do you have high-level emotional intelligence, problem-solving skills, and resilience? These traits can significantly boost future value and signal long-term success.

When figuring the NPV in relationships, we can't become obsessed with the numbers. At the same time, it's helpful to remember that the person you are considering for a date might not have reached their peak yet. Most people improve their financial picture over time. Conversely, you don't want to overvalue someone with little ambition or poor financial habits.

Assessing your Resources Score as well as that of possible partners means being honest with yourself and those you plan to move through life with. Look for signs of growth over time; the snapshot of a day or two doesn't give you an adequate picture of the important attributes of growth and consistency.

## Increase Your Resources Score

Fortunately, resource indicators, lifestyle choices, and intangibles provide massive opportunities to increase your resources. Education and training can raise your number, and developing discipline in your spending will bring your ranking up considerably. You can also build financial independence by acquiring assets like property or stocks. Budgeting, reducing and retiring debt, and learning to save all bring that resource number up. These factors also give you the power to work toward long-term goals, such as homeownership or retirement savings.

We might have a difficult time moving the other three Pillars of Dating scores by more than a point or two; however, there's no reason a three or a four can't become a seven or eight with some work and focus. We need a good balance in our four Pillars, and when resources are lacking, the other three have to be significantly above average to compensate. Financial difficulties put heavy strains on a relationship. So, be very honest with yourself. What's your NPV? What's your Resources ranking?

## Take Action

Answer these questions to give yourself a basic idea of where you fall on the Resources Bell Curve.

1. Are you satisfied with your current annual income? If not, does your ten-year plan realistically get you there?

   _____

   _____

2. Do you have adequate net worth outside your career? If not, does your five-year plan have a savings or investing goal to increase your net worth?

   _____

   _____

3. What do your spending habits look like? Do you spend within your means, avoid unnecessary debt, and refrain from impulsive purchases?

   _____
   _____

4. How's your work ethic? Do you show up for work (or school if you're still in college) every day? Do you take ownership of your job responsibilities and bring your best while working?

   _____
   _____

5. If you answered no to any of those questions, how will you improve your Resources Ranking?

   a. Get more education
   b. Set and stick to a budget
   c. Look for a better job
   d. Step it up at work
   e. Open a savings account and make regular deposits
   f. Open an investment account and make regular deposits
   g. Create a five-year or ten-year plan
   h. Other _____

6. According to the descriptions above, where do you fall on the Resources Bell Curve?

   _____
   _____

# CHAPTER TEN

# Assessing the Soul

*The true measure of a man is how he treats someone who can do him absolutely no good.*

—Samuel Johnson

Some things can be easily seen in a person—looks, appearance, how they carry themselves in a room. Our current dating culture knows how to reward these visible, swipeable traits. But this means we miss some of the most essential qualities in a person. Soul falls into this category of harder-to-detect qualities.

You can't swipe for Soul[IP]. Dating sites don't have a filter for it. No one lists this vital trait in their Tinder® profile, and it's difficult to capture through witty banter on a first date. The Soul doesn't jump out at you. It's not performative or something you "project." The Soul is something deep inside every person, and it reveals itself slowly, quietly, and most reliably when no one is watching.

In the DVP Quadrilateral, Soul represents the most sacred and difficult territory to grasp. A great actor can put a mask on a dark soul. This Pillar doesn't shout or show off. But it holds everything together.

A Soul full of light brings peace instead of pressure. It becomes a person's inner compass and source of calm. A wholesome soul is the very foundation of truth. The quality of the soul can easily be the difference between the person who shows up when it matters and the one who disappears when things get hard.

While Soul could have its roots in a belief system, it has less to do with what you believe and more with how your life aligns with what you claim to believe. Religious affiliation and spirituality aren't good measures of Soul. Rather, we evaluate this quality through the way a person forgives and serves. We see it in how we respond to emotional disruption and treat people who can offer us nothing in return.

Soul is more than a vague spiritual vibe. This real, living quality of character can be observed, measured, grown, and even rated, if you're willing to be honest about what it truly requires.

## The Dimensions of the Soul

Unlike the other pillars, Soul is multi-dimensional. Like a beautiful prism that allows light to shine through to create something beautiful, when someone's Soul is strong in each dimension, you can see the beauty without looking directly at them. The light that shines through leaves its mark all around.

You can't swipe for Soul. It's bigger than we can truly condense into words in a book. Soul has four key dimensions:

1. **Spiritual, or Vertical, Alignment:** The foundation of Soul begins with the idea of alignment. Alignment implies something governed not by preference but by principle. Choices, emotions, values, and relationships are tethered to something bigger than your

## Assessing the Soul

mood or the moment. In recovery, they call this their Higher Power. Others call it God, Jesus, truth, love, purpose, justice, or conscience. This alignment affects relationships, so we can use a **Relational Intelligence** scale to help us determine the health of our Soul. What values and beliefs guide your relationships? Some people call this a moral compass. It's rooted in where you align spiritually or religiously. Your capacity for kindness, forgiveness, and mutual respect lays the groundwork for this foundational tier. Spirituality and the idea of a spiritual connection are often important parts of a person's EQ. Some people place religious or spiritual alignment so high on the shelf that it becomes a showstopper when they sense an attraction in other areas but don't align with the potential date in this area. Most people value similarity and familiarity, especially in this area. This part of the soul drives dating sites like Christian Mingle, JDATE for Jews, and Muzz for Muslims. To rate this part of your Soul, ask, "Are you rooted in something greater than yourself? Do you live by values that transcend mood, culture, or convenience?"

> You can't swipe for Soul.

2. **Observed Presence / Community Impact:** Those with a Soul full of light live under a quiet but unwavering submission to something greater. Many modern dating metrics omit this essential component, our Emotional Quotient. This term, labeled EQ by Keith Beasley in 1987, allows us to recognize, understand, and manage our own emotions while being attuned to the emotions of others. Empathy, emotional regulation, and effective communication

create the foundation for EQ. People with a high EQ have the ability to listen actively and respond thoughtfully. They are better equipped to manage conflicts with patience and understanding and regulate their emotions without overreacting or shutting down. What is the felt experience of being around you? Do people feel calmer, safer, and more whole in your presence, or do they feel anxious, confused, or off balance?

3. **Virtue Profile:** Too often, Soul is most vividly revealed when a person's back is against the wall. You can learn a great deal from a person when their life starts falling apart. Do they consistently embody patience, forgiveness, humility, calm, and selflessness? Or do they veer into reactivity, self-protection, ego, or passive aggression?

4. **Motivation Sincerity:** A person with a Soul full of light will not be easily swayed by ego or impulse. Today's mood or perceptions about what others think don't move them too far off center. This is what makes Soul so powerful. It is not merely the absence of wrongdoing. It is the active presence of moral and emotional clarity. It's what you bring into a room before you speak. Those who prioritize integrity and demonstrate honesty with their actions and words will score high on the Soul Scale. They also have a commitment to fairness, patience, and compromise. Do you do good when no one is watching? Do you help people who cannot help you back? Do you sacrifice for the sake of love, peace, or integrity without applause?

When weighed together, these four dimensions give us the structure to assess Soul—not just theoretically but

## Assessing the Soul

practically. As we mentioned, you can't simply claim to have a great Soul. This Pillar is measured by how you consistently live when there's no applause. The sages of every great tradition—religious, philosophical, and poetic—all pointed toward the same indicators.

- Jesus spoke highly of the meek, merciful, and pure in heart.
- Buddha taught that hatred is not overcome by hatred, but by love.
- The Tao Te Ching praises water as the most potent force precisely because of its humility.
- Marcus Aurelius argued that virtue is the only true good.
- The Quran emphasizes that true love is based on respect, responsibility, and understanding.
- Desiderata reminds us to "go placidly amid the noise and haste."

And it's not just an ancient principle. The opening line of *The Purpose Driven Life*, written in 2002 by Rick Warren, contains a simple sentence that might be the single most accurate summary of Soul: "It's not about you."

This teaching, spread across continents, languages, and centuries, all contain the same truth: The quality of the Soul lies in the willingness to surrender. It is about selfless service, grounded conviction, and the ability to love without needing credit. And it is revealed most clearly through how you behave in the quiet, invisible corners of life.

## The Soul Score: Ten Levels of Internal Maturity

Below is the official Soul rating chart that I have developed. It blends ancient insight with modern behavioral cues. Like the other Bell Curves, most people fall between four and six in the Soul arena. The top tiers are rare. Not because they are unattainable, but because they require intentional surrender.

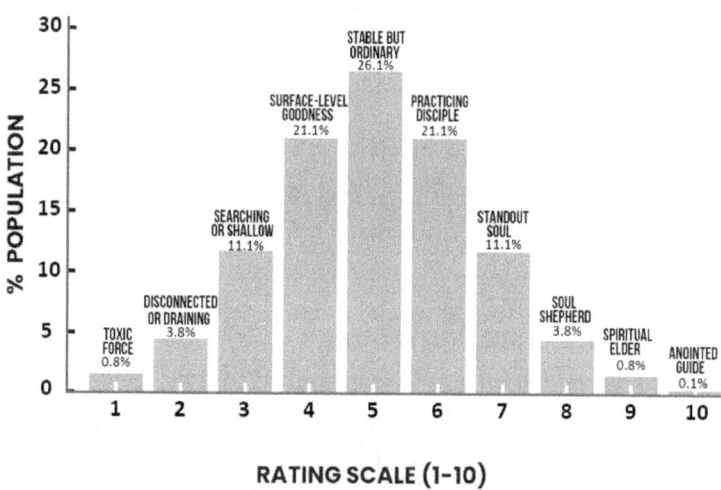

## Assessing the Soul

| Rating | | Spiritual Alignment (Vertical) | Observed Presence / Community Impact (Comparative) | Character Traits / Virtue Profile (Descriptive) |
|---|---|---|---|---|
| 10 | Anointed Guide | Lives in daily communion with a higher source or spiritual order; submits all ego. | Known across communities as a spiritual anchor, people seek them for healing, truth, or guidance; the rarest kind of person. | Radically selfless, peaceful under all conditions, never agitated, emotionally unshakable, ego-detached, deeply joyful, wholly focused on others' needs. |
| 9 | Spiritual Elder | Deep, disciplined spiritual devotion, denies self routinely, lives with sacred intentionality. | Recognized quietly as a moral compass, leads without striving, uplifts without pride. | Profoundly kind, emotionally still, slow to anger, not anxious or reactive, carries others' pain with grace, lives for purpose over recognition. |
| 8 | Soul Shepherd | Strong daily practices (prayer, study, meditation), puts mission above comfort. | Trusted in close circles, often mentors or intercedes for others' growth. | Humble, steady, not easily provoked, unshaken by ego threats, quick to listen, not self-focused, models calm under attack. |

| Rating | | Spiritual Alignment (Vertical) | Observed Presence / Community Impact (Comparative) | Character Traits / Virtue Profile (Descriptive) |
|---|---|---|---|---|
| 7 | *Standout Soul* | Regular spiritual discipline, clearly governed by higher principles, not trends. | Among the top few percent for soul maturity, presence is grounding and uplifting. | Exceptionally patient, emotionally grounded, not driven by self-interest, generous, calm in tension, never needy or defensive. |
| 6 | *Practicing Disciple* | Consistent spiritual rhythm and moral compass, submits regularly to a higher truth. | Respected by peers for steadiness and depth, others feel safe or at ease. | Kind with intention, emotionally regulated, rarely anxious or reactive, not driven by ego, begins to show absolute selflessness. |
| 5 | *Stable but Ordinary* | Believes in higher principles but with inconsistent spiritual practice. | Seen as a "good person," but presence lacks transformational impact. | Kind when it's easy, emotionally inconsistent under pressure, sometimes self-focused, avoids conflict more than resolves it. |

## Assessing the Soul

| Rating | Spiritual Alignment (Vertical) | Observed Presence / Community Impact (Comparative) | Character Traits / Virtue Profile (Descriptive) |
|---|---|---|---|
| 4 Surface-Level Goodness | Talks about values but lacks deep personal discipline or spiritual submission. | Socially likable but not spiritually grounded or emotionally trusted. | Kindness is conditional, often self-protective, easily rattled or annoyed, frequently anxious or self-preoccupied. |
| 3 Searching or Shallow | Expresses interest in more profound meaning, but avoids real surrender or alignment. | Comes off as "figuring it out," may inspire briefly but lacks consistency. | Emotionally unpredictable, generous only when praised, self-focused in growth and love, reactive, can't hold space for others. |
| 2 Disconnected or Draining | Lacks anchor in higher truth, ruled by ego, impulse, or emotional chaos. | Drains energy from others, known for being confusing, dramatic, or unstable. | Often anxious, defensive, self-serving, emotionally volatile, lacks empathy and peace. |
| 1 Toxic Force | Rejects or mocks spiritual and moral truth, governed by pride or nihilism. | Causes harm, fear, or emotional chaos in others, relationships often deteriorate. | Bitter, reactive, unstable, controlling, aggressively self-centered, spiritually deadening. |

## Why Soul Matters in a Relationship

Research from Dr. John Gottman shows that couples with similar worldviews handle conflict better and experience deeper connection. Ancient spiritual traditions emphasize the importance of a unified soul. In Corinthians 13:4-7, the Bible describes love as patient, kind, humble, and resilient—Soul qualities that define a strong relationship foundation.

But Soul is about more than religion. It's even more than finding a higher source of good. The soul is the essence of who you are. It encompasses your values, emotional depth, and capacity for meaningful connection. In relationships, the soul is where emotional and relational intelligence come into play. It's about kindness, empathy, shared values, and the ability to navigate challenges with resilience and grace.

The actual depth of Soul is found in selflessness and how willing a person is to sacrifice.

You see, true love requires sacrifice. I don't mean inviting abuse by removing healthy boundaries. Rather, this soul kind of love doesn't need to be first. It gives of itself for the greater good. Soul becomes vital in the DVP because it allows you to bring a sacrifice to the other Pillars.

A selfless Soul aligned with your Creator enables you to build a stronger Body. If you're addicted to food, alcohol, or drugs, when you strengthen your soul, you're willing to sacrifice the things you put in your body that don't make it better. It provides the strength to improve your Mind because you're willing to sacrifice time or money for education. A strong Soul helps discipline our spending as we sacrifice frivolous things to build our Resources.

The more you develop your Soul, the more willing you are to sacrifice your ego. Plus, when you practice this element of sacrifice when you're dating, you become more able to sacrifice for your mate and your children, your faith, and your values.

And when you start to get serious in a relationship, you'll find that this alignment of values in family, finances, faith, friendship, and future parenting is often the make-it-or-break-it moment.

The number one predictability marker for long-term compatibility is shared values. In short, if your souls don't align, nothing else will. A strong soul component creates the foundation for trust, intimacy, and long-term compatibility. And when you Date Like a Brand, you should explore this Pillar early in the relationship and look for someone who shares your spiritual or philosophical beliefs.

## Strengthening Your Soul Component

You can strengthen your body through repetitive muscle movement and your mind through study. But Soul? Soul grows through surrender, service, and silence.

For growth, your Soul needs daily alignment. Whether you use prayer, meditation, journaling, or solitude, you will grow this Pillar by doing good in secret.

The soul encompasses five intangible areas that can be strengthened with intentionality: empathy, values, forgiveness, emotional resilience, and spiritual connections.

Everyone can strengthen their Emotional Intelligence by practicing active listening. This means a shift in mindset. Instead of listening to respond and continually searching for the best way to answer, we listen to understand and learn to be comfortable with not having a response.

To cultivate empathy, we first need to understand our own emotions. What are your triggers? Why do some situations seem to push every button? It's difficult to develop empathy if you find yourself easily angered or offended. Some people need counseling to move through the emotions that hold them back. Getting to the root cause of these emotions that push others away can be extremely freeing.

Empathy also means we practice putting ourselves in others' shoes and listening without judgment. Consider how you'd feel if you were in their position. Think about their background. Does something in the other person's past influence their actions? By looking at every situation from various vantage points, you'll better understand different perspectives.

Recognizing and reflecting on our values will also increase our soul score. By identifying our core beliefs, we develop self-awareness to guide our decision-making. If we don't know our non-negotiables, we'll find ourselves in relationships that make us feel compromised. When actions align with values, we build integrity.

Many believe forgiveness and patience are purely for the benefit of others; however, holding on to grudges and being quick to anger can significantly impact our physical and emotional health. Unforgiveness increases cholesterol levels and our risk of heart attack and robs us of sleep.

Believe it or not, grudges can cause physical pain, high blood pressure, anxiety, depression, and stress.[10] Holding on to hurts can also fill us with resentment and negativity.[11] Releasing injustices can be one of the most challenging aspects of soul building. It often doesn't seem fair. We feel like we have a right to be bitter, angry, or stubborn. If the hurts run deep, you might need a coach or a counselor to help you. However, learning to let go and exercise patience, especially during conflicts and misunderstandings, will give you immense peace and increase your soul score significantly.

We learn emotional resilience through trials and setbacks. By looking at the difficult times through a lens of truth rather than worst-case scenarios, we can begin to manage stress and hard situations with grace. Each adversity gives us an opportunity to build coping mechanisms that will support

## Assessing the Soul

our emotional well-being. Breathing techniques, journaling, accepting the circumstances, reaching out to friends and family, practicing self-care, and finding your meaning and purpose can put you on the path to emotional resilience.[12]

Finally, your spiritual connections will prove invaluable when it comes to building the component of your soul. Many practices that nourish spiritual or philosophical beliefs, such as meditation, music, prayer, or reading, increase your soul score and have proven health benefits. They fight depression, lower blood pressure, and reduce stress.[13] Additionally, gathering with others who share your spiritual outlook and inviting them to challenge and strengthen your views will fortify your soul component.

A strong soul connection often becomes the glue that holds relationships together during tough times. Partners with high emotional intelligence can navigate conflicts with compassion. They see things from other perspectives, allowing them to find creative solutions. And shared values foster a sense of alignment and purpose, making the relationship more meaningful and enduring.

We build the integrity component of our Soul when we practice telling the truth, even when lying would make life easier, and forgiving people who haven't asked. Those with a strong Soul Pillar are detached from things that own them and seek wisdom that doesn't flatter but refines. Sometimes, it's good for us to hear hard but unpleasant truths about ourselves.

The person with a strong Soul is not perfect. They are simply principled, peaceful, and predictable in their compassion. These light-filled souls are consistent in their courage and beautiful in their selflessness. That's what makes a strong Soul rare, but not unreachable.

A strong soul will prove critical for emotional depth and alignment with the Love For Your Life. Still, we need all four Pillars to balance our DVP. The person with a high soul component might seem like great dating material, but if you have little compatibility in other areas, you'll probably struggle to build a sustainable relationship.

You can fake charm. You can fake ambition. You can even fake empathy for a while. But Soul eventually reveals itself. Soul is the part of your DVP that builds or degrades trust over time. It's the slow-burning fire that reveals whether a person is a safe place for love to land. And when you become someone whose Soul is trustworthy, you won't have to chase love. Love will recognize you.

And though the Soul learns to sacrifice, you'll discover that as you grow your Soul, your sacrifice will seem less sacrificial. A strong Soul will make the sacrifice feel natural. You'll never feel cheated. Instead, any sacrifice you make will give you more fulfillment, and others will notice.

You see, more than any of the other three Pillars, Soul always leaves a mark. It's the part of your brand people remember even after everything else fades.

## Take Action

1. Before giving yourself a six or more on the Soul scale, you must engage in an honest self-evaluation. Most people, by default, give themselves the benefit of the doubt. But to use this Platform effectively, we can't look for affirmation; our goal is accuracy because real growth only happens on the foundation of truth.

   Ask yourself a few basic questions:

   - Do I consistently do the right thing when no one is watching?
   - Do I offer help and love to people who can never repay me?

## Assessing the Soul

- Do I remain emotionally still when I'm misunderstood, criticized, or disappointed?
- Do people around me feel safer, more grounded, and more at peace because of my presence?
- Do I have an active spiritual rhythm—one that anchors me in values deeper than my ego?
- Am I free from addictions, or am I ruled by something I cannot say no to?

If you cannot answer "yes" to most of these, you might need some Soul-strengthening. Don't be too hard on yourself. It doesn't mean you're a bad person. And figuring out you need to work on this Pillar may be the most important realization of your life.

Your Soul score will prove even more subjective than your mind and body score, so take a few minutes to consider where you provide value emotionally and spiritually.

2. When you consider the five areas that define your soul component and judge them based on the questions you just answered, where do you rank yourself on each from one to ten?

- Empathy _____
- Values _____
- Forgiveness _____
- Emotional resilience _____
- Spiritual connections _____

3. The average of these will give you a number close to your Soul Score, so add them up and divide by five. _____

4. What number would you like this to be?

_____
_____


5. It's important to note that the area of spiritual connections generally can't be "improved upon." For some, this area of spiritual connection will equate to their religious preference or where they worship. For others, raising the overall score will increase the spiritual connection number, which will be enough. You shouldn't feel bad about your convictions in this area, but you want to be honest with yourself as you think about them. Which of the other four areas of your Soul would you like to improve first?

_____
_____


6. Would enlisting the help of a coach or counselor help improve your score? If so, when will you make the phone call to get started?

_____
_____


7. What other action steps do you need to take?

_____
_____

# CHAPTER ELEVEN

# Measuring the Strength of the Relationship

> *We have to recognize*
> *that there cannot be relationships*
> *unless there is commitment,*
> *unless there is loyalty,*
> *unless there is love, patience, persistence.*
>
> —Cornel West

In the world of marketing, we don't guess. We measure.

The best marketers don't just launch campaigns—they track how people respond. We use surveys, analytics, and consumer data to monitor the quality of the relationship between a brand and its audience. One of the most widely used tools is the Net Promoter Score (NPS). To determine our NPS, we ask a simple but powerful question:

*"How likely are you to recommend this brand to a friend?"*

The answer tells you everything about loyalty, satisfaction, and future potential. If you're not measuring your relationship with your customers, you're managing in the dark.

## Measure the Relationship

After we've done the hard work to build your brand and strengthen your DVP, why would you settle for running on chance? When you start to consider committing to another person (another brand), you've moved beyond selling to partnership. And just like in business, that partnership needs to be monitored, managed, and measured.

PDF[IP] is the tool we use to measure our Net Promoter Score. Based on Sternberg's Triangular Theory of Love, this framework measures the Passion, Decision, and Friendship in a relationship. Sternberg proposed that the healthiest, most enduring romantic relationships have these three things in common:[14]

- **Passion**: The physical component of the relationship—As the relationship progresses, is the physical attraction growing or fading? Is the relationship growing more intimate?
- **Decision**: The mind compatibility of the relationship—Are you both on the same page with your vision for the future? Are your plans for children, lifestyle, careers, and future similar?
- **Friendship**: The long-lasting part of the relationship—Do you genuinely enjoy being with each other? Do you feel safe and energized after you spend time together?

These three dimensions work like a triangle. Though they don't always show up equally, and they may rise and fall over time, if one side weakens substantially, the shape—the relationship—becomes unstable. The PDF Triangle becomes our Relationship Scorecard. It gives us a means to analyze the strength of the bond of the relationship beyond how good your partner looks on paper. It allows us to quantify love with grounded insight rather than guesswork.

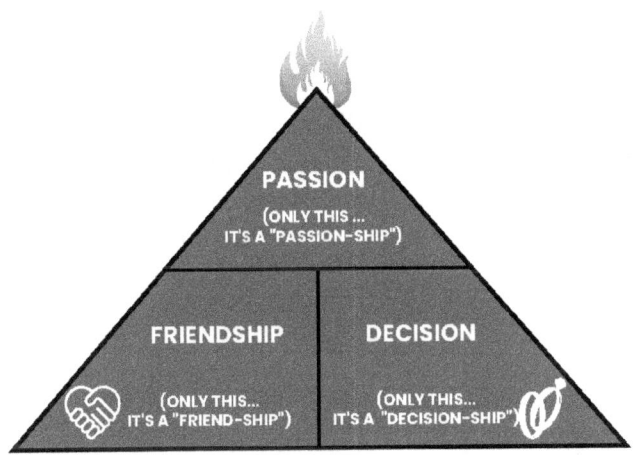

Each dimension of the PDF has a ten-point scale, much like the DVP Score. Understanding your PDF allows you to assess your relationship the way brand managers evaluate performance by looking at what components are average, which parts are exceptional, and where the partnership is at risk.

A five rating in any of the three areas indicates an average relationship. Ten means part of the partnership is excellent, and a one indicates an extreme breakdown or absence of that element.

There is a major difference between the DVP Score and the PDF Scale. While an average score in the DVP means you're much like most of the population, a five in PDF isn't acceptable. Just like in marketing, an average performance rating is a warning sign. Average will not keep customers loyal, and it won't sustain a partnership either.

The reason the divorce rate remains a consistent 50 percent is because too many people coast through their relationship, assuming a five in friendship and a four in decision-making are passing. While it's functional, that level of PDF is not fulfilling, and eventually, the striving becomes exhausting.

To sum it up, while your relationship will survive a five in one or two areas of DVP, maintaining a five average in PDF is not a sustainable strategy. Healthy relationships, like successful brands, do the work. They innovate, communicate, and recommit. They don't assume; they measure and adapt. So let's look at the scale to see how your partnership measures up.

> **SITUATIONSHIPS VS RELATIONSHIPS:**
> • JUST PASSION? THAT'S A PASSION-SHIP — HOT BUT HOLLOW.
> • JUST DECISION? THAT'S A DECISION-SHIP — PLANNED, NOT FELT.
> • JUST FRIENDSHIP? THAT'S A FRIEND-SHIP — SWEET, BUT STALLED.
> **FOR A RELATION-SHIP, FOCUS ON SUFFICIENCY IN THE WHOLE PDF.**

## The Passion Scale

The Passion scale measures emotional and physical intensity. More than the other two, Passion may fluctuate as the demands of life change; however, if it remains at a five or below for a significant amount of time, you'll need to give this area extra attention in order to keep your partnership healthy.

# Measuring the Strength of the Relationship

| Rating | Description |
|---|---|
| 10 | A rare form of lasting passion. The emotional and physical connection remains vibrant, soulful, and continually renewed over time. Few couples sustain this level—but it's possible when emotional depth and desire evolve together. |
| 9 | Very high attraction and chemistry. Desire rekindles easily and often. |
| 8 | Frequent and fulfilling intimacy. Connection stays exciting over time. |
| 7 | Above-average passion. You make an effort to stay attracted and connected. |
| 6 | Some spark remains. You're still attracted, but not always expressive. |
| 5 | *Average couple:* Intimacy happens but feels routine or strained. |
| 4 | Passion has declined. Intimacy feels obligatory or faded. |
| 3 | Attraction is fading, and you feel disconnected physically. |
| 2 | Minimal desire. Intimacy is avoided or feels strained. |
| 1 | Passion is absent. Resentment or repulsion may be present. |

## The Decision Scale

The Decision Scale measures your commitment and long-term clarity. Many couples are together without a clear alignment on their future. This mindset that settles for average sets the stage for an unsustainable relationship.

| Rating | Description |
|---|---|
| 10 | Total mutual clarity. You've chosen each other with shared goals and strategy. |
| 9 | Long-term commitment has been tested and affirmed. |
| 8 | Strong mutual intention and daily alignment. |
| 7 | Clear and growing commitment. You're investing on purpose. |
| 6 | Defined commitment, but future plans need clarity. |
| 5 | *Average couple:* Commitment exists in name, not vision. |
| 4 | Commitment is ambiguous. One or both feel unsure. |
| 3 | Fluctuating commitment. Breakup-and-makeup cycles are common. |
| 2 | One partner is emotionally exiting. |
| 1 | No real commitment. One or both are done. |

# Measuring the Strength of the Relationship

## The Friendship Scale

The Friendship Scale measures emotional safety and companionship in the relationship. Being "teammates" without developing a deep level of friendship leaves your partnership average. You want more than to merely "do life together."

| Rating | Description |
|---|---|
| 10 | Deep friendship. Total trust, comfort, and laughter. |
| 9 | Exceptionally close. You genuinely enjoy each other. |
| 8 | Consistent companionship and openness. |
| 7 | Above-average friendship. You talk, laugh, and connect. |
| 6 | You work well together. Some depth, but not fully open. |
| 5 | *Average couple:* You coexist but don't always connect. |
| 4 | Friendship has faded. You don't talk deeply anymore. |
| 3 | You feel emotionally isolated or judged. |
| 2 | Communication is minimal. Trust feels broken. |
| 1 | No friendship. Conflict, distance, or bitterness dominates. |

## The Scorecard

Use this scorecard to evaluate your relationship. Where does it stand today? What would you like it to look like next year?

| SIDE OF THE TRIANGLE | 1–3 (Low) | 4–6 (Functional) | 7–10 (Thriving) | Your Score |
|---|---|---|---|---|
| **Passion** | Weak or absent. Physical and emotional intimacy has faded. | Some spark remains, but it's inconsistent or routine. | You maintain a strong and expressive connection. | [   ] |
| **Decision** | No clarity or fading commitment. | You're "together," but the vision is unclear. | You've chosen each other. Mutual clarity exists. | [   ] |
| **Friendship** | Emotional distance or mistrust. | You function, but rarely connect on a deep level. | You feel safe, seen, and supported. | [   ] |

**Total Score (Max = 30):** [     ]

## What It Means

| Score | Interpretation |
|-------|----------------|
| 25–30 | **Exceptional:** A strong, intentional relationship with full alignment. Keep nurturing. |
| 21–24 | **Healthy:** Minor imbalances. Continue investing in weak spots. |
| 15–20 | **Functional, Not Fulfilled:** You're surviving, not thriving. Focused work is required. |
| <15 | **At Risk:** Critical gaps. Time for honest evaluation and change. |

## Take Action

Growing brands don't coast to success. They refresh, relaunch, and revisit their strategies. Love is no different. An annual check-up of your PDF will prove invaluable if you want a sustainable, growing relationship. Those couples who've been married for fifty years and still enjoy each other's company didn't get there by accident.

At least once a year, review your PDF and ask a few questions:

- Where are we thriving?
- What are we overlooking?
- Where do we need to intentionally invest more?

Even seasoned marriages can benefit from taking this inventory on a regular basis. The best relationships don't happen by accident. They're built, tracked, and renewed. Use the PDF to help you stay strategic, accountable, and aligned.

# CHAPTER TWELVE

# The Dating Value Proposition Lifecycle

*The earlier you make the right choices and the tough sacrifices, the longer you will have to enjoy the benefits, BUT... the opposite is also true.*

—Vince Hudson

As you move through your dating years, it's vital to remember you are a brand. This means your dating lifecycle mirrors the trajectory of a brand in the market. Just as products move through stages—Introduction, Growth, Maturity, Deceleration, and, if done right, Renewal—people go through similar phases in their personal and romantic lives.

Each stage has specific indicators and brings changes, both intentional and inevitable. Additionally, every phase offers unique strategies to move your brand closer to finding the Love For Your Life. But unlike consumer products, the dating marketplace places different demands on men and women based on their DVP mix and unique strengths. Depending on your gender and which areas of your DVP are strongest, your market value may peak earlier or later.

This creates a natural tension. Men and women of similar ages are often at different stages of peak demand at the same time. But that's where strategy matters. Whether your DVP peaks early or late, and whether you're male or female, your dating strategy must evolve as you move through the DVP lifecycle[IP].

## Gender Plays a Role

We also have to acknowledge the underlying historic shift in gender dynamics. Historically, men held more power in dating and marriage because they controlled financial resources. Prior to the 1990s, the expectation was simple: a man provided, and a woman nurtured.

But today, women outpace men in higher education and many career paths. Consider these shifts:

- In the 1970s, 60 percent of college students were men. Today, 60 percent of college students are women.[15]
- Men's workforce participation has declined, while women's has increased.[16]
- Though the median real wage for women has increased by about 30 percent since 1980, wages for working-class men have stagnated. The real wage for men has actually dropped by 3 percent, making traditional male provider roles harder to maintain.[17]
- As gender roles have changed, many men struggle with purpose and confidence in relationships. At the same time, women don't need marriage for financial stability.

One thinker whose perspective has deeply shaped my own is Professor Scott Galloway. I've had the opportunity to meet him in person a few times, and each time, I walked away in awe, not just of his intellect, but of how sharply

## Date Like a Brand

he sees patterns in society that many of us only feel. His insights on gender, economics, and relationships cut through the noise with clarity and courage.

In particular, his collaboration with social scientist Richard Reeves on "Marrying Up and Marrying Down" has influenced how I think about modern dating and the complex forces reshaping how we choose partners today.

As Galloway and Reeves explain, we're living through a historic reversal. Women now dominate higher education and are advancing across nearly every professional metric. That progress is worth celebrating, but it also brings a new challenge. While many women remain open to partners without degrees, they still want someone who is economically and emotionally viable.

In today's market, women may be more likely to "marry down" in education, but rarely in earnings. Meanwhile, men who lack economic stability or a clear sense of purpose are increasingly falling behind—not just in careers, but in relationships, family formation, and overall well-being. The result is a growing marital class gap that is reshaping the dating landscape in ways we're only beginning to fully understand.

Galloway often says the most important decision you'll make isn't what company you work for but who you choose to build a life with. I couldn't agree more. That's what drives my passion to help people make that decision differently, not just emotionally, but strategically. In a world where the rules of love are shifting, success in dating, like in business, starts with knowing your value, refining your offer, and learning how to position yourself in a marketplace that rewards clarity, confidence, and consistency.

That means these gender trends have to be figured into your performance numbers, especially for those in the more mature stages of the Dating Brand Lifestyle. The rules that our parents adapted to no longer apply.

# The Dating Value Proposition Lifecycle

Though women now have more options and control over their futures, they still seem to be expected to carry the emotional load of the relationship. This can be exhausting. That's why the PDF and DVP become vital tools for a career woman.

Men carry the burden of understanding that women of the twenty-first century place higher expectations on relationships than their mothers and grandmothers. Most are looking for men who are at least as ambitious as they are. These women want partners, not someone to take care of. This means your gender, as well as your DVP and PDF, influence the DVP Lifecycle.

Dating performance is about clarity and calibration, not luck. So, let's break down the five stages of the lifecycle. Understanding these stages allows you to think strategically, align your actions with your objectives, and navigate the dating market with intention.

## The Five Stages of the DVP Lifecycle

1. **Introduction** is the first stage in the branding lifecycle. A product enters the market with different goals and strategies than a brand that's already made a name for itself. The dating lifecycle has a similar beginning.

   Eighteen- to twenty-five-year-olds typically make up the introductory phase of the Dating Brand Lifecycle; however, if you've waited until you have a career to begin dating or never identified your DVP, you might spend a short time in this stage at a later date.

   - **Key Characteristics**: Fresh, inexperienced, and exploring independence.
   - **Objective**: Establish your presence and build awareness of your value proposition.

In this stage, you're building the foundation for your future; it's marked by experimentation and self-discovery. This phase lets you develop your value proposition in mind, body, soul, and resources while beginning to understand what you seek in a partner.

**Current Value Proposition:**

- **Mind**: Expanding through education and life experiences.
- **Body**: Likely at its peak, with youth and vitality in your favor.
- **Soul**: Still developing, with emotional intelligence and values becoming clearer.
- **Resources**: Limited, as you're just starting your career.

Women whose DVP leans heavily on Body or Soul often find this to be a phase that gives them high attention. Men who are driven by an attraction to youth, beauty, and emotional spark create a high market demand.

Men find this to be more of a building phase. Because most are still developing Resources and Mind, they have relatively little market power unless their DVP includes standout charm or physical appeal.

**Strategic Considerations:**

- **Women with early DVP peaks** should balance attention with intentionality; short-term attraction is not a long-term strategy.
- **Men should invest heavily** in education, personal growth, and resource-building. Their time is coming—but patience is key.

# The Dating Value Proposition Lifecycle

- **Both:** Use this time to experiment, refine your identity, and begin shaping the DVP you want to mature with.

2. **The Growth Stage** usually occurs when a person is between twenty-five and thirty-five. During these years, we build our value as we find a career, become better at making wise choices, and learn from the follies of our youth.

    - **Key Characteristics**: Gaining experience, increasing confidence, and growing your value proposition.
    - **Objective**: Maximize your potential while exploring serious relationships.

    This is where your value proposition evolves significantly. In addition to advancing your career, you're also refining your social skills and solidifying your values. Many people begin to look for more serious relationships during this phase, especially if they aim to start a family.

    Women whose DVP focused on Body previously may notice a shift. Those entering the introductory stage may become competition. For women who have higher DVP scores in Mind, Soul, or Resources, this is a stage of rising power.

    Men come into clearer demand here, especially as Resources and Mind begin to shine. This is a transitional phase for men. They move from being overlooked to being actively pursued, especially by women seeking stability.

    **Changes in Value Proposition:**

    - **Mind:** Sharpening through work and life challenges.
    - **Body:** Still attractive, but the youth edge softens slightly.

- **Soul:** Deepening, more emotionally intelligent.
- **Resources:** Increasing with career development.

**Strategic Considerations:**

- **Women:** Determine whether you're in your peak market moment or building toward a later one. Don't rush or settle. Choose strategically.
- **Men:** Stay the course. Keep building. Demand will continue to increase if you sustain growth.
- **Both:** Clarify values and relationship goals. Start filtering partners through long-term lenses, not just vibes.

3. **The Maturity Stage**: Between the ages of thirty-five and forty-five, most people begin to reap the rewards of their years of hard work. Your achievements start to speak for themselves, and your confidence levels have increased significantly.

    - **Key Characteristics**: Stability, clarity, and peak alignment of resources and soul.
    - **Objective**: Secure a meaningful, long-term relationship that aligns with your life goals.

    Men often reach their prime during this stage, especially if they have a DVP rich in Resources, Mind, or Soul. Their market power is high, and options are plentiful—particularly with younger partners looking for maturity and stability.

    Women who led with Body in the early stages may have to deal with reduced demand unless they've worked to build up their other areas. Those whose DVP Strengths are Mind, Soul, or Resources will probably hit their stride.

## The Dating Value Proposition Lifecycle

**Changes in Value Proposition:**

- **Mind:** Highly developed; wisdom becomes attractive.
- **Body:** Slightly declining but can remain strong with effort.
- **Soul:** Often at its most grounded and centered.
- **Resources:** Peaking for many.

**Strategic Considerations:**

- **Women:** If your DVP is more long-game (career, intellect, soul), this can be a golden era. Prioritize partners who align with your emotional and lifestyle maturity.
- **Men:** Avoid becoming arrogant or superficial in success. Substance and character are what differentiate good partners from temporary trophies.
- **Both:** Consider relationship timing. If children or legacy matter, this stage is critical for making clear, life-aligned decisions.

4. **The Deceleration Stage** begins sometime around or after one's forty-fifth birthday. Many begin to think seriously about what retirement will look like, and health issues related to age may start to present themselves.

- **Key Characteristics:** Major life transitions, reassessment of values, and potential midlife crises.
- **Objective:** Address unmet expectations and rediscover personal and relational purpose.

The Deceleration Stage often brings emotional turbulence, especially if you haven't found the Love For Your Life yet.

Men who relied too heavily on Body or Resources may struggle if health, looks, or work slow down. Those who cultivated Soul and Mind can still attract powerfully.

Women may feel the weight of external biases around age and appearance. But for those who have invested in internal value, this can be a stage of unmatched depth and clarity.

**Changes in Value Proposition:**

- **Mind:** Rich with wisdom and perspective.
- **Body:** Declining unless managed proactively.
- **Soul:** Deep, refined, often the most attractive quality.
- **Resources:** Stable or winding down, depending on the path.

**Strategic Considerations:**

- **Women:** This is your moment to lead with depth. Stop competing with youth; start leaning on meaning.
- **Men:** If your DVP was over-indexed on wealth or youth, you'll need to evolve fast. It's time to become relationally valuable.
- **Both:** Reassess your story. If past relationships didn't work, reframe them. Don't chase youth; chase growth.

5. **The Renewal/Sustain Stage** finishes the Dating Lifecycle, assuming we don't get stuck in stage four. By taking an honest look at our DVP and being strategic about what we can do rather than sinking into the despair of what we can't, this stage allows us to thrive through reinvention. Fortunately, this stage can begin as early as the day after we recognize deceleration.

# The Dating Value Proposition Lifecycle

- **Key Characteristics**: Resilience, adaptability, and finding joy in new pursuits.
- **Objective**: Rebuild confidence, adapt to new realities, and maintain relevance.

This stage is about reinvention, second acts, and deeper truths. Whether it's rediscovering yourself after a divorce or pursuing new hobbies in retirement, this phase is an opportunity to adapt and thrive.

This stage is about second acts and deeper truths. Whether post-divorce, widowed, or simply in a new life chapter, you have the power to reconnect with yourself and attract aligned partners.

Women often find unexpected empowerment in this stage, especially in communities and cultures that value emotional maturity and shared purpose.

Men finally discover the attraction of emotional availability, consistency, and a purpose-filled vision.

**Changes in Value Proposition:**

- **Mind:** Focused and wise.
- **Body:** May be less of a draw, but health still counts.
- **Soul:** Often unmatched.
- **Resources:** Repositioned for impact, legacy, and lifestyle.

**Strategic Considerations:**

- **Women:** Don't dim your light. You're not behind—you're refined. Seek alignment, not validation.
- **Men:** You have more than enough—if you lead with the right things.

- **Both:** This is the soul-mateship era. Choose someone who matches your growth and values. And never forget—love evolves.

## Playing to Your Life Stage

Understanding the Dating Lifecycle and aligning your actions with your objectives proves key when you start to Date Like a Brand. Each stage offers unique opportunities and challenges that impact Dating Performance. Success comes from playing to your strengths and evolving your value proposition.

Women who want children may find the earlier stages more critical to achieving their objective. Men often wait until the maturity stage to find their Love For Life because they have more time to maximize their value proposition, but it may also limit opportunities. Waiting means you're more likely to find a partner with children from a previous marriage or find yourself raising children long into your retirement years. You also limit your ability to experience life with a younger partner.

By thinking strategically and aligning your value proposition with your stage, you can navigate the dating market with confidence, clarity, and purpose.

## Understanding the Two Crisis Cycles of the Lifecycle

Every brand faces pivotal moments in its existence. These turning points allow the brand to test its strategy and form a long-term identity. In the same way, every person goes through two major psychological and emotional inflection points that shape their relationship journey—the classic quarter-life and mid-life crises—and we need to understand how to leverage them when it comes to dating.

# The Dating Value Proposition Lifecycle

The quarter-life crisis hits just about the time we pass our twenty-fifth birthday. Nearly everyone starts to question career choices and wonder if they should be married already. If they married before this crisis, they may begin to wonder if they settled too soon.

For women, it can be extremely intense because it collides with the awareness of their biological clock. Additionally, a woman's DVP traditionally peaks just about the same time, which brings even more pressure, whether or not the woman plans on having children.

This crisis can make men feel as though they've fallen short. Though they are still under construction, they'll wonder if they're growing into the man they imagined.

The more familiar mid-life crisis hits about age fifty, right after most men have reached their peak. This is the brand plateau for your life. Most of us have scaled by now. Our house and resume look impressive, we're married, and we have children. By now, you've lived long enough to have a track record, and you're starting to face the consequences of previous mistakes. It's difficult to begin rebranding after this crisis. You have too much history. The midlife crisis becomes a day of reckoning.

Both the quarter- and mid-life crises require a reevaluation of our DVP. While many want to run from them, these are perfect times to be honest with yourself and strategize for the future. Many people run from these periods instead of looking at them as times of growth and gates to the next level of their DVP. Being aware that these crisis levels exist can help us avoid damaging relationships and stunting our growth as we try to emotionally deal with the questions these milestones produce.

You might wonder why women peak earlier than men. After age thirty-five, the women's curve on our graph gradually declines. This is primarily driven by reproductive timing and the cultural emphasis on youth and appearance. Meanwhile, the men's curve's peak coincides with career advancement, financial maturity, and emotional growth.

We also must remember that our DVP is our General Market Score. The number changes depending on the room. If you're entering a space filled with your specific target audience, you might find your score rises by a point or two. It's the same you, but from a different perspective. For example, a Korean-American man who primarily dates Korean-American women in an age range close to his own is now competing with a smaller segment of the population. This decrease in competition can have a significant positive impact on your DVP.

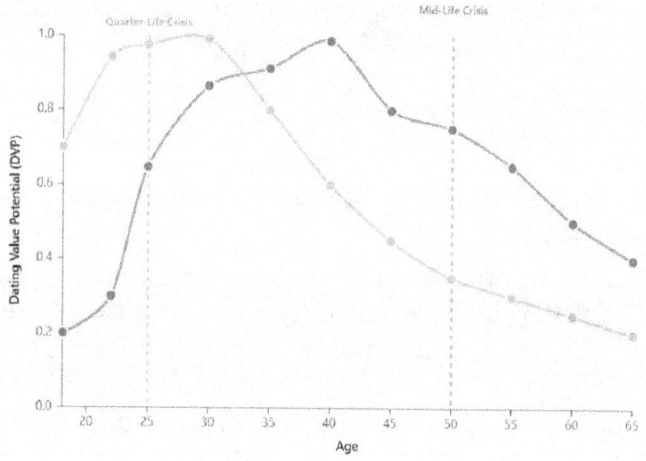

**DATING BRAND LIFECYCLE: DVP VS. AGE (WITH LIFE CRISES)**

The same applies to a fifty-year-old woman who feels average compared to a national pool that includes twenty- and thirty-year-olds. She could potentially be exceptional within her actual target market. Likewise, a man earning $100,000 might be a ten on the resources scale in places where the cost of living is lower, but score close to a six in someplace like San Francisco. Context matters.

## The Dating Zone Matrix

Brands use two-by-two matrices to evaluate opportunities by bringing together two key variables—such as market size and competitive advantage—to decide where to invest. The top-right corner is always the goal: where potential and payoff align. In dating, the same logic applies.

This matrix combines the two crucial factors we've defined to help you prioritize where to invest your time and emotions.

- DVP: The person's overall value—mind, body, soul, and resources.
- PDF: The strength of the relationship itself, based on chemistry, commitment, and compatibility.

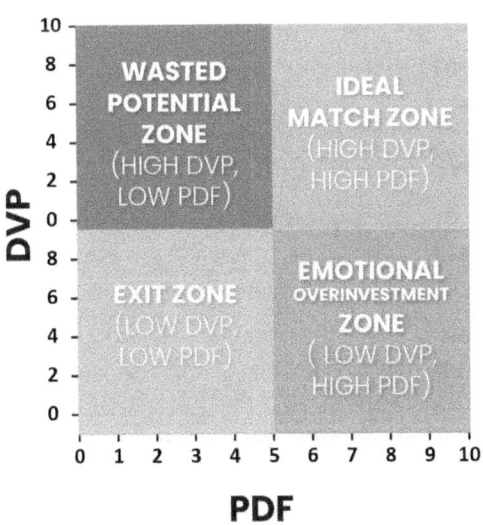

By placing a dot where the two components intersect, you can determine the strength of the relationship and understand where your effort is going.

- ✅ Top Right—If your dot falls in this square, you're in the **Ideal Match Zone.** We also call this the Loyalty zone. There's strong personal value and deep mutual connection. This is a partner with long-term potential.
- ❗ Top Left—The **Wasted Potential Zone.** These potential partners' high DVP makes them look great on paper, but the relationship lacks glue. The low PDF means emotional disconnection or misalignment could lead to burnout or loss of interest.
- 💭 Bottom Right—The **Emotional Overinvestment Zone.** High PDF will make you feel deeply connected, but a low DVP shows a practical or holistic value may be missing. You may love hard, but long-term compatibility could be lacking.
- ❌ Bottom Left—The **Exit Zone.** Your relationship has low value as well as low connection. It's time to ask: "Why are we even here?" There's little foundation for anything lasting.

## Take Action

Intentional dating means you need to measure and review your metrics. In other words, the actions in this chapter, like the action steps in many of the previous chapters, need to be repeated with every potential relationship. Plus, they'll need to be reviewed on a regular basis to be sure everything is still performing well. To see the impact of the Dating Zone Matrix, review your past relationships.

## The Dating Value Proposition Lifecycle

1. Reflect on your relationships that have ended

    a. On a scale of 1–10, how would you rate each person's **DVP** (Mind, Body, Soul, Resources)? _____
    b. On a scale of 1–10, how would you rate the **PDF** (Passion, Decision, Friendship) between you? _____
    c. Plot that on the matrix. Which zone were you in?

    - Wasted Potential Zone (High DVP / Low PDF)
    - Emotional Overinvestment Zone (Low DVP / High PDF)
    - Exit Zone (Low DVP / Low PDF)
    - Ideal Match Zone (High DVP / High PDF)

    d. What do you wish you'd done differently in that situation?

2. Assess your current relationship (if applicable)

    - Where would you place it today on the DVP-PDF matrix?
    - If it's not in the top right quadrant, what needs improvement?

        - **Their value**
        - **Your connection**
        - **Both**

3. Spot your pattern

    - Have most of your relationships landed in the same quadrant?
    - What does that tell you about your **dating habits or blind spots**?

4. Set a goal

    How will you move **up and to the right** in your next or current relationship?

    - ☐ Improve how you choose partners (target higher DVP)?
    - ☐ Strengthen the relationship itself (build PDF)?
    - ☐ Both?

## CHAPTER THIRTEEN

# Let's Play: The DVP Market Chips Game

*Love is a game that two can play and both win.*
—Eva Gabor

*The right person will love all the things about you that the wrong person was intimidated by.*
—Anonymous

I have a game I like to play with those who come to me for dating advice. I call it the DVP Market Chips Game[IP]. It allows the prospective dater to realistically identify their DVP and become more aware of what they're looking for in a partner. Let's face it, you can't hit the target if you don't know what the bullseye looks like.

I've created an online version you can access at DateLikeABrand.com, or you can go old school and grab twenty poker chips or pennies, a pencil, and a piece of paper—you could even use twenty pretzel sticks.

After you gather your twenty chips, draw a four-square on a piece of paper. In each of the boxes, write one of the Four Foundational Pillars of Dating. We will use this diagram to determine what you should look for in a partner.

Begin by putting five chips in each of the four areas. That's what your ideal partner's DVP would look like if he or she ranked exactly average on each bell curve.

As you know, few have an even spread across the Pillars. So, you're going to have to move the chips around. This will give you a visual of what you're really looking for on a date.

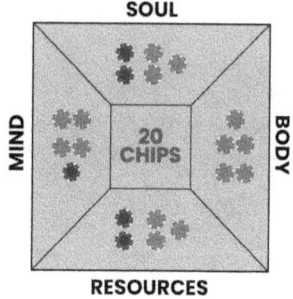

CHIPS GAME SPREAD OUT 20 CHIPS ON GAMEBOARD OF THE 4 PARTS OF DVP

Which of the four areas is most important to you? You'll want some extra chips there. This means you have to take some from the Pillar that matters least. But you don't want to take any to zero. Each component has some weight.

If you want a partner who scores a seven in Mind and Soul, you have to decide how much you're willing to sacrifice in Body and Resources to get there. You might only be able to give Mind a six if you want at least a four in Resources.

This exercise can be beneficial because you don't want to waste your time with someone with only two chips in the Mind square if your ideal partner needs six. If the person you're considering going out with is a good match in Mind and Body—areas easier to evaluate from a glance or a few minutes of conversation—it might take a first date or longer to uncover their Soul and Resources rankings.

And remember, it's not just someone with a low ranking you want to watch out for. If someone ranks an eight in

LET'S PLAY: THE DVP MARKET CHIPS GAME

Resources, but you are looking for someone who scores a six, you might find that person places more emphasis on work or money than you will be comfortable with over the long haul.

## I Need More than Twenty Chips!

Many people I work with have difficulty playing the game with only twenty chips. While they don't mind putting four chips in one of the squares, they want five to eight in each of the others. More than one person has complained, "Twenty just isn't enough!"

What if I told you I'm willing to give you a few extra tokens to spread around?

The secret to earning extra chips is in your own evaluation. Let's take a second four-square, but this time you get as many chips as you need to match the levels you scored yourself when we talked about bell curves.

Did you score more than five (or above average) in any of the Four Pillars? If so, add that number of chips. If you scored less than five in any area, take that number away. And don't forget to reevaluate your chip count if you make improvements.

After you fill in your own foursquare, add up your chips. For every chip over twenty, you can add a bonus chip to your ideal partner's four-square. Do you have twenty-three chips total? Add three chips to your potential partner's four-square. Maybe you made it to twenty-seven? You can add seven chips to that first foursquare.

The higher your DVP, the more you can expect from someone you date. Every time you do the work to move your DVP up a chip, you can add a chip to any square in your ideal date's foursquare.

## Your Perceived Market Worth

As you complete the chip game, I want to remind you that this exercise does not define your self-worth. You shouldn't feel bad if you only have two or three chips in one area.

This simple exercise can not possibly evaluate your total worth. It doesn't take into account your Unique Selling Proposition or the hard-to-define parts of your personality. The purpose of these chips is to help you see yourself like the world sees you before they get to know you, to show you your *perceived* market value. It allows you to honestly evaluate places you can improve and be realistic about the kind of person you're most likely to attract.

Knowing your Perceived Market Worth gives you a starting point. Remember, you want to look for someone who has a similar Perceived Market Worth, but how can you do that unless you're aware of your own?

## Take Action

After you have completed your self-assessment and your Partner Brand Ideal Match, take photos of each so you have them on your phone and can refer to them often.

1. Are they comparable in overall score?
2. Are there area you need to be more flexible on?

## Let's Play: The DVP Market Chips Game

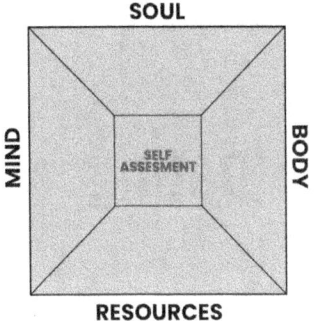

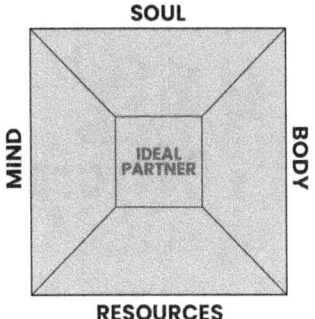

For the best experience, try these "chip" exercises for FREE at DateLikeaBrand.com. It is AI-enabled to give you customized feedback.

# CHAPTER FOURTEEN

# Performance Dating

*Work smarter, not harder.*
—Allan F. Mogensen

In modern marketing, "performance" is more than just a buzzword; it's a requirement. Creativity isn't enough. Brand management demands results. Campaigns must convert. Budgets must perform. Without performance, the brand dies, no matter how good the product is.

Dating is no different. Your emotional budget—your time, energy, and effort—is finite. You can't keep pouring into people who don't convert into clarity, commitment, or compatibility. Welcome to Performance Dating, where we learn to track progress, spend wisely, and clarify the difference between attention and value.

After they determine their prime market and make certain their product is reaching their target audience by evaluating the Place, Price, and Promotion, marketers run their decision through a list of metrics to determine the Performance of their efforts. Cost per Acquisition (CPA), Return on Ad Spend (ROAS), and conversion rates top the list of determining factors. But how does this translate into the dating landscape?

## Performance Standards

Brands begin by creating a measurable structure. They identify Key Performance Indicators (KPIs). In dating, without these metrics, we rely on vibes or gut reactions. And while these aren't always wrong, laying out specific **KPIs** can take the guesswork out of our Performance Dating.

- On a scale of one to ten, how aligned is this person with your ideal traits?
- How quickly and consistently do they follow up?
- Do they initiate? Do they reciprocate effort?
- Do you feel calm or confused after each interaction?

Answering these questions honestly about each person you date can give you vital information about whether to invest more time and effort into that person. These few indicators can give you a preview of your chances of a successful partnership.

Online companies often use **Funnel Tracking** as a marketing tool. They offer apps, books, and free information to get your email address, and then they send a series of messages to introduce you to their lower-priced products or services, and after they've invested some time and effort, they show off their big-ticket item. Some folks jump off the email chain immediately after they receive their free offer, and others opt out after the first sales pitch, but a few stick around until the final offering. And a percentage of those even buy!

Marketers evaluate their promotion methods by looking at how many people drop out after each campaign. They track the funnel so they can make tweaks in their marketing and enhance the performance of their advertising strategy. In dating, we can do the same thing.

- **Top of Funnel:** At the top of the funnel, you're just getting noticed by others in the dating field. Plus, you begin to look at who's entering your dating world and by what means. Did you find the person on a dating app, social media platform, professional engagement, or other means? How many looked like genuine prospects before your first date? Do you need to change your Place or increase your Price to make the pool a bit clearer?
- **Middle of Funnel:** Those who make it through the second and third date pass through to the middle of the funnel. Did any prospects not call after the first date? Were you ghosted? Do those who made it to this point look like potential Loves For Your Life? Does their DVP match your ideal? If not, do you need to tweak your promotion a bit?
- **Bottom of Funnel:** At the bottom of the funnel, we find those who have the potential for sustained relationships. Only a few will make it this far; that's why it's called a funnel—much bigger on the top to accommodate the masses and smaller on the bottom because you've narrowed down the field.

A Relationship Funnel can be useful for evaluating your Place, Price, and Promotion. This formula allows you to diagnose drop-offs and increase your odds of finding the right person at the bottom of your funnel.

**A/B Testing** allows marketers to test how different promotion tactics attract different customers. They learn which methods fit their target consumers best. The same thing applies in dating. Because you've identified your Prime

Prospect, you can apply A/B testing to determine which behaviors attract different types.

- Shift your "promotion strategy." You might add new photos or put a different bio on each online platform. In person, consider changing the time or place of your dates. Track whether or not your prime prospect type noticed each move.
- Evaluate your Strategy. The goal in A/B testing is to determine what attracts the type of partner you want, not simply find a person who likes you.

## Don't Use Vanity Metrics

Brand strategists all understand the dangers of **Vanity Metrics**. Clicks make you feel good. Followers and likes boost confidence. However, not every click, like, and follow converts to a sale. Similarly, chemistry doesn't equal compatibility. Just because the person made you feel good about yourself on the first date doesn't mean it's a lasting relationship. We want to avoid Vanity Metrics in dating:

- *There was a spark between us.* Beware of fast flings that spark but don't scale.
- *He (or she) says all the right things.* Enthralling words without consistently executed actions should raise red flags.
- *They are so entertaining.* Dates that are entertaining but don't involve deep conversation won't move you closer to commitment.

Finally, marketing experts watch out for **Low-Value Activity (LVA).** Sometimes, promotional campaigns cost too much and deliver too little. We have to make certain we don't spend time on people who don't move the relationship forward or show meaningful reciprocal feelings. Three questions will help us determine the performance of our investment.

- **Am I confusing attention for investment?** If the relationship never moves past the talking stage and doesn't demonstrate a desire to move forward, they might not be invested in a partnership.
- **Does this person fluctuate between hot and cold, leaving me guessing?** Do you find yourself overperforming to compensate for the other person's cold times? Is this person truly making me a better person, or am I simply hoping they will change?
- **Could my time be better spent nurturing a different relationship?** Often, rather than being in a relationship or friendship, you find yourself in a "situationship." Do you feel as though you're making sacrifices to maintain the relationship? Just because the situation presents itself doesn't mean it's the best place for you to be.

Each of these tests can help us determine whether the time and effort we put into the relationship are valuable.

## Take Action

1. Where does the person you're dating fall on your DVP scale?

_____

_____

_____

2. On a scale of one to ten, how much time and effort does the relationship take?

3. Do you confuse attention with investment?

4. Does the other person leave you guessing?

5. Would you be better off nurturing another relationship?

6. Grab a notebook and create a dating journal. Keep track of how you feel after each encounter, including dates, phone calls, messages, and other interactions. Evaluate each encounter—did it move the relationship forward?

# CHAPTER FIFTEEN

# Factors That Impact Performance Dating

*When someone shows you who they are, believe them.*
—Maya Angelou

*Strategy without tactics is the slowest route to victory. Tactics without strategy is the noise before defeat.*
—Sun Tzu

The strategies in dating aren't any more cut and dry than those used in marketing. Several factors will impact the metrics we discussed in the last chapter. Your age, lifestyle, the effort you put into raising your DVP, and the choices you make as you proceed in the relationship all play into the success of your Performance Dating.

## The Role of Sampling

Marketers know that offering a small product or service sample creates interest and intrigue. Consider your last trip to

## Factors That Impact Performance Dating

Costco. They love to give you a bite of their products—just enough to whet your appetite. That's the magic of sampling. It entices the customer to invest, to purchase the full product. If they enjoy the sample, they'll want more!

When it comes to dating, there's no escaping the elephant in the room. Sex is an undeniable part of human connection, and naturally, people have a million questions about it.

- Does sex early in the relationship help or hurt?
- When is the "right" time?
- How does sex impact my decisions and the viability of the relationship?

Questions surrounding the topic constantly swirl in the minds of daters. And while there's no one-size-fits-all answer, we can turn to the tried-and-true marketing structure of sampling to guide our thinking.

Imagine the impact if Costco handed out full boxes of cookies instead of just one per customer. Sure, some people might love the product and come back for more, but many wouldn't feel the urgency to make a purchase. Why? Because they already got what they wanted for free. They're satisfied—at least temporarily—leaving no pressing reason to commit to buying. In dating, sex works the same way.

When you give someone everything upfront—sex, intimacy, and emotional vulnerability, in addition to your tremendous DVP—it's the same as Costco giving away the whole pack of cookies. The person you're dating might enjoy it, but they haven't had to invest anything to earn it. Without investment, there's no emotional buy-in. And without buy-in, there's no foundation for a lasting relationship. We can actually apply the same principle to moving in together.

In marketing, we use a structured scale to determine the likelihood of someone purchasing our product or service.

It ranges from Definitely Would Buy to Definitely Would Not Buy. The dating landscape offers a similar continuum to consider as we practice Performance Dating. Each time we consider dating, this scale comes into play in our mind as well as the mind of our possible date. A caution: Marketers typically only count the top box, "definitely would" or "5", and a small percentage of the "4" and "Probably would" responses in their forecasts. You should follow a similar approach. When people get to know each other, very rarely do their ratings move from the middle Might or Might Not (or Below) up to the top 2 ratings.

## "MARRIAGE INTENT" (SCALE)

| RATING | MARRIAGE INTENT (DWM) |
|---|---|
| 5 | **DEFINITELY WOULD MARRY**<br>FULLY ALIGNED FOR LONG-TERM LOVE |
| 4 | **PROBABLY WOULD MARRY**<br>STRONG POTENTIAL WITH SHARED VALUES |
| 3 | **MIGHT OR MIGHT NOT MARRY**<br>COMPATIBLE IN SOME WAYS, UNCLEAR FUTURE |
| 2 | **PROBABLY WOULD NOT MARRY**<br>CHEMISTRY PRESENT BUT POOR FIT LONG-TERM |
| 1 | **DEFINITELY WOULD NOT MARRY**<br>CLEAR MISALIGNMENT ON CORE FOUNDATIONS |

We start trying to discern intent in the Pre-Assessment phase. However, dating offers a complication we don't have in marketing. If we're going to Date Like a Brand, we have to consider a second relationship continuum. While the first measures marriage potential, the second gauges hook-up possibilities. A potential mate will "play with" you but not with a long-term goal. Which continuum the date falls on and where he or she falls determine intent; however, when we skip the sampling process, we muddy the waters.

## "PLAY WITH" INTENT (SCALE)

| RATING | "PLAY WITH" INTENT |
|---|---|
| 5 | **DEFINITELY WOULD PLAY WITH**<br>TOTAL FUN, IRRESISTIBLE CHEMISTRY |
| 4 | **PROBABLY WOULD PLAY WITH**<br>HIGH FLIRT FACTOR, EXCITING ENERGY |
| 3 | **MIGHT OR MIGHT NOT PLAY WITH**<br>CURIOUS BUT NOT COMPELLING |
| 2 | **PROBABLY WOULD NOT PLAY WITH**<br>LOW INTEREST, MINIMAL SPARK |
| 1 | **DEFINITELY WOULD NOT PLAY WITH**<br>BORING OR UNCOMFORTABLE VIBE |

When we give our date the entire box of cookies—have sex too soon—we only give our potential partner the information they need for the second scale. They don't have time to assess you on the first one. With their immediate desire fulfilled, they might not stick around long enough to decide if you'll commit, and you can't judge their intention either.

Marketers understand that customers value what they invest in. When a man has to work for a woman's time, attention, and affection, he becomes emotionally invested. The effort he puts forth creates a sense of value around the relationship. If everything comes too easily, there's no challenge, no effort, and ultimately, no lasting connection.

When you wait to have sex, it forces the other person to focus on your DVP—your mind, body, soul, and resources—without being distracted by physical intimacy. Plus, you have time to observe the other person's behavior and determine if they're genuinely interested in building a relationship or just looking for a hookup. It's impossible to test the metrics we discussed in the last chapter if our judgment has been compromised by a prematurely intimate relationship or a joining of community property.

With the whole pack of cookies in their hands, they have time to sample other "products" on the shelf. On the other hand, if you offer just a taste—a bit of your humor, intellect, and kindness—they'll be intrigued. They'll want more. A sampling makes the potential partner come back hungry for what you have to offer. And in the meantime, they'll have to invest their time, energy, and effort to get it.

## Time and Testing

Timing is everything when it comes to sex and moving in together. Despite what the movies would have you believe, there's no strict rule or specific number of dates to guide our timing. Instead, we want to create the right conditions for emotional investment to ensure both parties are on the same

## Factors That Impact Performance Dating

page. Waiting gives you time to take the relationship through three steps:

1. **Observe Consistency:** Do their words and actions align over time? Someone who is serious about you will show consistency in their behavior.
2. **Clarify Intent:** Open communication is crucial. Early conversations about relationship goals can help distinguish casual interest from genuine investment.
3. **Patience:** People may initially rate you as "Might or Might Not Marry" because they need more time to assess compatibility. Patience also allows you to gather more data and make informed decisions.

Sex should only come after you answer yes to a few questions.

- Have they shown genuine interest in my DVP (mind, body, soul, and resources)?
- Are they putting forth effort to get to know me beyond the physical level?
- Have I observed their behavior long enough to know their true intentions?

In order to Date Like a Brand, we have to view sex as more than a mere transaction. We have to see it as an important step in building a relationship—a step that requires investment and follows sampling.

First, let them taste the best parts of our mind and soul to create desire, foster emotional investment, and ensure you have aligned intentions. Allowing time for mutual interest and effort to build doesn't mean you're playing games. Instead, it's a sign of building a foundation for something real and strong.

So, the next time you're faced with the question of "when," remember that sampling is a powerful tool. Give enough of yourself to intrigue, but never the whole pack of cookies. I like to say, "Don't sample the whole Costco Cookie. Some people go to Costco like they're at Red Lobster." Wait until the other person invests. Let them earn while you earn, and let the relationship grow authentically. Because love, like a great product, is worth the effort.

## Factoring in the Two Systems of Marketing

Dating strategically, like marketing strategically, means we learn to leverage the power of the subconscious. When I worked at Samsung®, we took a deep dive into market research, trying to understand why certain customers remained so loyal to Apple®. We knew Samsung devices had objectively better specs, screens, and cameras. Our software was more customizable, and sometimes, we even offered better battery life. On paper, choosing Samsung was a slam dunk.

Yet, many people clung to Apple.

At first, we tried to rationalize it. "They're just used to it," or "It's about the ecosystem," or "They don't know better."

But nothing we could come up with explained the emotion we heard when people talked about their iPhones. This was more than brand loyalty. It went much deeper.

We finally realized Apple had mastered what psychologists call System 1 thinking. This is the immediate, intuitive, and emotional response people feel even before they know why they enjoy something. It's based on first impressions, physical attraction, chemistry, and gut feelings.

### System 1 (Fast, Emotional)

- First impressions
- Physical attraction

## Factors That Impact Performance Dating

- Chemistry
- Gut feelings

Apple was sexy.

More than the phone, people loved the *feeling* of owning it. The minimalist packaging, the aluminum edges, the blue bubble in the group chat, and even the story people told themselves when they took it out of their pocket.

While Apple products triggered desire in milliseconds, Samsung forged ahead, trying to win the spec war. They focused on the long-term, thought-provoking, and rational. Samsung marketing was grounded in System 2 thinking while Apple dominated System 1.

But then something interesting happened. Samsung launched bigger phones. At first, it confused people. Even some of us internally scratched our heads. After all, wasn't the whole point of these all-in-one computer/phone combos portability and sleekness? Surely "easier to hold" would take the day.

Turns out that logic didn't matter as much as we thought.

"Bigger is better" struck a primal nerve. It needed no explanation. People felt it. Holding a larger phone made them feel powerful, productive, and premium. Samsung had found its place in the instinctive, emotional realm—another win for System 1.

This realization became a turning point for me. Everything clicked. From phones to dating, **humans don't make decisions rationally—they rationalize them later.**

Daniel Kahneman coined the phrases System 1 and System 2. They operate side by side in every human brain. System 1 works on the subconscious level. It gets your heart racing. Without hesitation, System 1 swipes right and smiles uncontrollably after a first kiss. It quickly evaluates facial symmetry, voice tone, smell, and energy, and it reacts in milliseconds.

System 1 says things like:

- "There's just something about him."
- "I don't know why, I just can't stop thinking about her."
- "It doesn't make sense, but I'm drawn to them."

System 1 doesn't care about logic. It works on emotional pattern recognition and is heavily influenced by your attachment style, upbringing, and even your unresolved wounds.

## System 2 (Slow, Rational)

- Compatibility
- Life planning
- Shared values
- Trust and communication

System 2 kicks in later. It evaluates and plans. This is the conscious part of you that takes time to make rational, logical, and strategic decisions. System 2 thinks about things like compatibility, life planning, shared values, trust, and communication.

This stage asks questions:

- "Can I build a life with this person?"
- "Are our values aligned?"
- "Do I trust them with money, decisions, and future kids?"

System 2 is the voice of your future self. While System 1 focuses on chemistry, System 2 will home in on compatibility. This part of your brain reads the resume and listens for patterns. It does the mental math.

Though it's working right alongside System 1—albeit at a slower pace—too many people ignore System 2 until

## Factors That Impact Performance Dating

the dopamine wears off and the emotional illusion starts to crack. Most of us have lived through the regret of giving those logical voices in our heads a backseat to the screaming feel-good hormones.

Dating strategically means we understand this principle and pay attention to how it influences our choices. In marketing, we call System 1 *sizzle* and System 2 *substance*. When choosing your target audience, you need to factor in the sizzle and substance.

- What kind of person excites the System 1 part of your brain? What patterns show up in the people you find instinctively attractive? Which folks create a little sizzle?
- What does the System 2 voice tell me I should look for in a healthy long-term partner? What do I consistently see in people who seem to have substance?
- Where do these two Systems overlap, and where do they clash?

Because System 1 often follows your attachment style rather than your values, it's vital to know your attachment style and determine whether or not the sizzle is really good for you. What feels like chemistry might be a trigger.

Fortunately, the *Date Like a Brand* framework—the 6 Ps Platform, as well as your USP, DVP, and PDF—has the power to strengthen your response to System 2. This structured strategy can help you date with clarity, not just craving.

System 2 isn't "better" than System 1 or vice versa. But relying only on System 1 is like buying a sexy sports car without considering whether you like to take five friends on long road trips. Relying only on System 2 is akin to marrying someone because they "check the boxes," even if there's no spark.

True relationship success comes when the person your heart wants is also the person your head trusts when chemistry (System 1) meets compatibility (System 2). Passion without purpose burns out. Purpose without passion dries up.

There is an important and controversial aspect in mate selection that I didn't bring up during the Body part of the DVP discussion (which ultimately impacts how someone might rate the Body dimension). But now that we're in a world where individuals freely choose their own partners, this aspect becomes critical: producing quality offspring. This is a subconscious and conscious dynamic that straddles both System 1 and System 2 thinking. Our biology is constantly scanning for partners whose physical traits suggest strong, competitive, attractive children—that's System 1 firing before we've even formed a sentence. But once the attraction is triggered, System 2 steps in to validate it with thoughts like "We'd make beautiful kids," or "Our children would be smart and tall." That's why the Body dimension isn't just about current attractiveness; it's also an implicit prediction about the future value of the DNA you're choosing to combine.

> Success comes when chemistry (System 1) meets compatibility (System 2).

## The Role of "Consultants" in Dating

In business, it can be exceedingly helpful to hire consultants to point out spots in the business that could be tweaked. The outside perspective helps us work through blind spots and biases. Unfortunately, not all consultants are created equal—in business or in dating.

In business marketing, we look for consultants who specialize in our particular niche. Someone who understands the ins and outs of vehicle marketing may not serve the restaurant world well. Additionally, we have to remember that consultants offer insight, not ownership. They can bring flashy presentations, recommendations, and workshops, but when the campaign hits or fails, they will not be the ones reporting to the executive team. The marketing department will have to live with the results.

Dating is no different. This means we need to truly evaluate the consultants we listen to.

Everyone has asked their friends for advice at one time or another, but have you ever considered that you've essentially hired an unpaid consultant? And just like in brand strategy, we have to filter their opinions and comments.

Every consultant brings their own perspective to the table. We all have a worldview, a set of experiences, and a value system that influence the advice we give. This means when our friends offer advice, we have to look at it through the lens of their bias.

A friend who has been cheated on may have trust issues. Their advice might include "never trust them again" policies. Another person who married at age twenty-three may not understand your standards at age thirty-five, and your friends who have become disillusioned with love may secretly—even unknowingly—root for your heartbreak.

Plus, we need to remember that not everyone wants our relationship to work. Some people are more comfortable with your struggle than your success. A few will fear you'll become less available if you find love, while others compare your happiness with their own pain. Others watch you grow with envy because it reflects their stagnation. Most of the time, they won't even realize they're bringing this bias to their advice. It's not that they want to sabotage your relationship, but they're human.

As the brand manager, it's your job to protect your product. We have to filter every piece of advice with an open mind. That means we consider our consultant's words, not dismissing them simply because they sting. But at the same time, we aren't afraid to bypass even the most friendly suggestions when we realize they don't fit our brand.

The best way to evaluate each piece of advice is to filter it through these four questions:

1. **Does the consultant live the kind of relationship life I respect?**
   Track records matter. If your friend excels at relationships, you might want to put more weight on their suggestions. If they bring a string of failed relationships to the table, do you really want to rely heavily on their advice?
2. **Are they advising you based on your Dating Value Proposition or projecting their own?**
   Friends naturally judge potential partners through the lens of their own dating value and options. Someone with a lower DVP may tell you to "stop being picky," while someone with a higher one may set unrealistic expectations. Make sure their advice reflects your position in the dating market—not theirs.
3. **Is your friend invested in your happiness or their influence?**
   Some people have a high need to be right. Beware of advisors who can't celebrate your joy if it means they are wrong.

If you constantly find yourself in toxic situations, you might need a professional. Therapists and counselors often offer new perspectives, and fortunately, a well-trained counselor will leave their own biases at home.

You might also find great advice from other experts. Webinars, podcasts, and even TikTok clips can help you reframe your patterns and look at your relationships from new points of view. However, these kinds of consultants have to be taken with context.

For example, a viral TikTok clip or a famous podcaster might say, "If he wanted to, he would." While that's true, nuance matters. If your significant other shows up in eighty other healthy ways but falls short in communication, we have to decide if that one shortcoming really outweighs the eighty great qualities. That's why we have to understand our own DVP. Is communication the make it or break it in your DVP, or do you have an avoidance tendency that looks for excuses to push good people away?

It's important to put even professional advice in context. Remember, you are the Chief Marketing Officer of your brand. Consultants may come and go, but you own the campaign. We must understand ourselves and hold our knowledge up against the insight others bring.

When you're confident in your brand, you can welcome feedback. You might not always use it, but you trust yourself to filter it. When it comes to advice, we must learn to listen, reflect, filter, and then launch. Most importantly, we must never outsource the final decision.

## Take Action

As I've said since the beginning, understanding yourself is key to the *Date Like a Brand* principle. Paying attention to these Performance Dating Factors can help you have greater success as you begin to look for the Love For Your Life with intention.

1. Where are you in the Dating Brand Lifestyle?

2. How do you think your gender affects the way you perceive the dating landscape?
   _____
   _____

3. Without setting specific performance indicators, it's easy to skip sampling or move from sampling to sex too soon. What standards will guide your Performance Dating sampling?
   - _____
   - _____
   - _____

4. Who do you consult with before or after your date? Does this person have a track record worth replicating?
   _____
   _____
   _____
   _____

5. Reflect on how offspring influence your attraction.
   - System 1: What instinctive traits pull you in when you imagine future children (e.g., height, symmetry, athleticism, skin tone)?
     _____
     _____

   - System 2: What are the long-term implications of those traits (health, social mobility, opportunities), and do they align with the legacy you want to create?
     _____
     _____

# CHAPTER SIXTEEN

# The Four Agreements of Dating Like a Brand

*The best way to find out if you can trust somebody is to trust them.*
—Ernest Hemingway

*Do the best you can until you know better.*
*Then when you know better, do better.*
—Maya Angelou

In both life and leadership, principles matter. One of the most powerful principles I've ever encountered comes from *The Four Agreements* by Don Miguel Ruiz. I've used Ruiz's book not just personally but professionally. I have even gifted copies to my marketing leaders as a compass for how we lead, build, and communicate. Why? Because principles that work in life almost always work in marketing, and dating is no exception.

Brands live or die by the values they consistently demonstrate. In the same way, relationships thrive or fail based on how well we live out foundational truths. Don Miguel Ruiz's

Four Agreements (Be Impeccable with Your Word, Don't Take Anything Personally, Don't Make Assumptions, and Always Do Your Best) are timeless truths for navigating complexity with clarity and grace.

I've taken the liberty to reframe the author's work to create a foundation—a brand code—for modern dating. When we show up with emotional strength, integrity, and resilience, we make our relationships stronger, and something that's become fragile in the twenty-first century—a marriage partnership—has an increased survival rate.

## Agreement 1: Be Impeccable with Your Word

Most people look for integrity in brands they support. They want the company's words to match their actions, and when they do, they build a relationship and trust. Your words matter even more.

In branding, inconsistent or misleading messaging breaks consumer trust. A brand that overpromises and underdelivers quickly loses loyalty. But unless it's a tremendous lie or simply a bad product, people will keep going back. In dating, the slightest breach of trust can erode a person's feelings of emotional safety and destroy a relationship permanently. In dating and marketing, trust compounds through consistency.

Being impeccable with your word means honoring what you say and communicating from a place of truth, never manipulation. It means you are Consistent, Authentic, and Transparent.

To build trust, you must:

- **Say what you mean and follow through.** If you say you'll call, call. It doesn't matter how tired or busy you are; if you care, you will consistently reply to texts and do what you say. Reliability is attractive.

- **Present yourself honestly everywhere.** Don't enhance your dating profiles with half-truths, filtered photos, or inflated résumés. People appreciate authenticity in conversation and expectations.
- If you're seeing others or not looking for something serious, **make that part of the conversation** in the first moments of the relationship. Transparency helps us avoid miscommunication or perception of deception. Respect begins with clarity.

## Agreement 2: Don't Take Anything Personally

Dating can be hard on a person's self-esteem. But here's an important truth: the way other people respond to you is more about them than it is you. Don't take someone moving on as rejection or a judgment on your value. Think about it. Some people prefer chocolate ice cream. That doesn't lessen the value of vanilla ice cream. When a customer chooses one product over another, it seldom has anything to do with brand flaws; the decision generally indicates a personal preference. Innovative brands don't spiral when a click doesn't convert; they iterate. What feels like rejection isn't a referendum on your worth.

To avoid taking things personally, you'll need Resilience, Empathy, and Boundaries.

- Every date gives you information to improve yourself or narrow your target audience. When someone opts out of the relationship, we need to look at it as data, not damage. Resilience reminds us that not every person will be the right fit, and that's okay.
- Remember that everyone carries baggage. Fear, trauma, timing, and more shape behavior more than we realize. Understanding that our past shapes our

view and our personality can help us look at the perceived rejection with Empathy towards the other person rather than Emotion. When someone ghosts you, you might be tempted to focus on figuring out how you messed up. Instead, recognize and empathize with the fact that their silence reflects their emotional immaturity or readiness for a relationship.
- Protect your peace at all costs. Don't overanalyze someone else's decisions. Healthy Boundaries will help you stop when you blame yourself for a break-up.

## Agreement 3: Don't Make Assumptions

Assumptions are always dangerous. They're akin to trying to read minds. In dating, assumptions can be deadly. They cause misalignment, unmet expectations, unnecessary heartache, and unrecoverable strains on the relationship.

In marketing, assuming your audience's needs without testing or listening leads to failed campaigns. Great brands test, listen, and respond. These principles hold true for dating as well: ask, don't guess, clarify your intentions, and seek understanding.

- Never assume someone wants the same thing you want or guess what a period of silence means. Ask questions. "Are you open to a relationship?" "Have you been busy the last couple of days?" Guessing will always end badly.
- Be upfront about your own expectations. Clarifying, like transparency, takes the guesswork out of the relationship, and your candor gives your potential partner permission to be clearer. Silence leads to story-making. For example, you might assume

someone is serious about the relationship because they invited you to meet their friends or family. But unless you've discussed the level of the relationship, it's merely a story you're telling yourself. Don't leave room for someone's imagination to run wild. Value clarity over fantasy.
- If something feels off in the relationship, address it early. Directness prevents disappointment. By seeking to understand, we open the door to more open and honest conversation.

## Agreement 4: Always Do Your Best

You can't control the outcome of a date any more than a marketing guru can control the result of a campaign. However, we can control the effort. Even when things don't go perfectly, showing up fully, giving without expectation, and learning from challenges will ensure we leave no regrets and preserve our confidence.

- Being present and engaged is vital, from the first date to your sixty-second wedding anniversary. Showing up fully will prove key to a lasting relationship.
- Kindness and effort are not currency. We must learn to put forth the effort with no expectation of reciprocation. Giving without expectation can be difficult to practice at first, but it will prove invaluable as you build a relationship.
- When things don't work out, extract insight instead of carrying regret. What could you do differently to be your best self? Did you choose to date someone with a DVP far different than your target audience? Learning from challenges means we evaluate what appears to be a failure and go forward better

equipped. If a date doesn't lead to a second, and you know you brought your kindest, most attentive, and respectful self, count it as a win! The most impressive brands learn from their misses.

## FOUR AGREEMENTS OF DATING LIKE A BRAND

**1. BE IMPECCABLE WITH YOUR WORD:**

- SAY WHAT YOU MEAN AND FOLLOW THROUGH
- PRESENT YOURSELF HONESTLY
- RESPECT BEGINS WITH CLARITY

**2. DON'T TAKE ANYTHING PERSONALLY:**

- RECOGNIZE IT ISN'T ABOUT YOU
- FOCUS ON EMPATHY OVER EMOTION
- SET HEALTHY BOUNDARIES

**3. DON'T MAKE ASSUMPTIONS:**

- SAY WHAT YOU MEAN AND FOLLOW THROUGH
- PRESENT YOURSELF HONESTLY
- RESPECT BEGINS WITH CLARITY

**4. ALWAYS DO YOUR BEST:**

- SHOW UP FULLY
- GIVE WITHOUT EXPECTATION
- LEARN FROM CHALLENGES

# The Four Agreements of Dating Like a Brand

## Take Action

Dating is full of false starts, disappointments, euphoric highs, and awkward exits. These Four Agreements aren't merely a coping mechanism; they're your competitive advantage. Keeping them in the forefront as you Date Like a Brand will help you navigate rejection, foster honest communication, prevent misalignment, and operate from a place of self-respect. In branding and love, integrity always wins. Your word, your consistency, your intention, and your mindset will become your reputation.

Answer these questions to determine whether or not you are living the Four Agreements.

1. Do I present myself authentically in how I show up and communicate?

_____
_____
_____

How do I need to improve?

_____
_____
_____

2. How do I respond to rejection or silence? Do I spiral or stay grounded?

_____
_____
_____

How can I learn to take things less personally?

3. What assumptions am I making in my current romantic situation?

4. What questions do I need to ask to bring clarity to the relationship?

5. Did I bring my best self to my last interaction, regardless of the outcome?

6. How can I improve at always being my best?

# PART THREE

## GO TO MARKET

# CHAPTER SEVENTEEN

# The Six Launch Gates of True Love

*Faith is taking the first step
even when you don't see the whole staircase.*
—Martin Luther King Jr.

*Every new beginning comes from some other beginning's end*
—Seneca

Before I introduce people to strategic dating, they often assume love just happens—or doesn't. But if you've ever worked on a major brand launch, you know that nothing successful happens by accident. Whether you're launching a product or a partnership, it requires clarity, testing, investment, and timing. Love is no different.

In brand strategy, we use gates to evaluate whether something is ready to move forward. More than simply milestones, these rigorous checkpoints test for alignment, readiness, and market fit. In relationships, gates serve the same purpose:

they help you move at the speed of wisdom, not emotion. These are the Six Launch Gates of True Love[IP].

*Failure to Launch* is more than just the name of a funny movie. It's also a problem many face as they navigate this era of finding a lifelong partner. For most people, it feels like walking on a beach, fighting the waves and the sand. So, let's walk through each gate—from internal readiness to public launch—so you know what it takes to build not just chemistry but a co-branded love worth sustaining.

## Before the Gates: Get Market-Ready

As we discussed, embracing who you are and polishing those areas where you can improve are vital. These things need to be accomplished before you move into the dating world.

As you lay the foundation for your dating brand, you'll need to:

- Clarify your DVP and make certain you have a balanced understanding of your Mind, Body, Soul, and Resources.
- Reflect on your attachment style and emotional patterns.
- Understand your family formation values and the kind of future you want to build.
- Polish your packaging—your appearance, energy, and personal presentation.
- Define your minimum standards for a partner—the must-haves, dealbreakers, and growth areas.

Self-readiness is not perfection; it's preparation. It gets you ready to stop reacting to what's around you and start selecting based on what's within you. But don't get stuck in perpetual prepping. Eventually, every product has to start to scout the market.

THE SIX LAUNCH GATES OF TRUE LOVE

## Gate One: Discovery—Swipe Left and Pay Attention to Chance Encounters

In marketing, Gate One is the top of the funnel—your front-end marketing and early exposure. At the Discovery Gate, we look for qualified leads, gather early insights, and learn what the dating market has to offer.

In this phase of dating, exclusivity is not expected or required. You won't be making any investments. You will meet new people, explore profiles, exchange messages, and engage in casual flirting. Contact will include swiping, messaging, video calls, quick coffee dates, blind dates, and other connections that don't require deep investment. This Gate allows you to collect DVP clues and see who sparks your curiosity without commitment.

Culturally, you discover:

- Men often enjoy lingering at this Gate. It keeps their options open without any emotional investment.
- Many women prefer to speed through this stage, especially if they're tired of surface dating.
- Women with avoidant attachment styles may want to stay at this Gate. It offers the freedom to stay independent and unbothered.

Think of it like this: When a brand launches a new product, it begins with light consumer awareness. They start running ads, and social buzz builds, but they don't expect any bulk orders. They're just testing the water.

To move past this Discovery Period, you must meet at least these criteria:

- You've identified at least one person worth seeing in real life.

- You've exchanged enough messages to create curiosity and mutual interest.
- You're ready to stop browsing.
- You're aware that swiping is *not dating*, and excitement is not the same as investment.

Once someone begins to stand out, you're ready to move into Validation. Is what you think you see actually there?

## Gate Two: Validation—Real-Life Dating Without Commitment

The Validation phase is like a product demo. You've seen the packaging, read the reviews, and now you're trying it in your environment. You're still not exclusive—you may be validating more than one person—but you're no longer guessing. You're watching for a few signs:

- Consistency between words and behavior.
- Early signs of PDF: Does the relationship have Passion? Has the other person made an intentional Decision to spend time with you? Do you enjoy being with them in the realm of Friendship, beyond the romantic moments?
- How does the person interact in different settings: quiet dinners, group hangouts, errands, or road trips?
- Your own comfort level—do you feel more like yourself when you're with them?

Culturally, you'll see:

- Men often stall in this phase because there's enough connection to enjoy the perks of dating without the responsibility.

- Many women want to leave this stage quickly. They've seen enough to make an investment, and they want to lock in.
- Avoidant attachment types may feel safest here, regardless of gender. They can be emotionally present but stay distant enough to retreat if necessary.

To complete Gate Two:

- You've had three to five real-life interactions.
- You've observed the other person's behavior in public and private.
- You've experienced each other in a variety of moods and situations.
- You and one other person from your non-exclusive field are open to exclusivity and have real potential across DVP and PDF dimensions.
- You've evaluated the relationship against the Definitely Would MarryIP and Definitely Would PlayIP parameters.

After you check those boxes, you're ready to stop playing the field and test one relationship in full.

## Gate Three: The Test Market—Exclusive Dating, Strategic Evaluation

This Gate moves us into the most strategic and vulnerable place in the relationship. In the Test Market phase, your relationship becomes exclusive through a mutual decision to give it a try, together and out in the open.

In business, test markets aren't casual. Brands pour resources into launching a product in select cities, knowing the world is watching. The exposure is real. The investment is real. The feedback is real.

Your relationship needs the same kind of commitment.

This is the first time you and your partner go all-in. You leave the comparison pool behind and date each other with full focus. You're not playing anymore, you're building. Assessment moves from compatibility to viability.

This is the longest Gate in most relationships. As you pass through Gate Four, you'll encounter:

- Real-world trials: Missed flights, bad days, family conflict, and health scares.
- Decisions that reveal true values and resilience.
- Opportunities to fully assess each other's DVP stability and growth potential.
- Stressors that will test your PDF strength.
- All four emotional seasons:
    - Spring: Bonding, fun, and optimism.
    - Summer: Deeper merging and higher heat.
    - Fall: Flaws show up, and we settle into routines.
    - Winter: Stress rises, and passion fades. Can you withstand the cold?

Gate Three isn't just about surviving stress; during this phase, we have to answer every major relationship question so we're ready to enter the next Gate.

To complete the Test Market, you must resolve:

- **Finances**—Compare budgets, review debt, review saving styles, and discuss lifestyle expectations.
- **Geography**—Where will you live? Who will relocate? You need a plan.
- **Roles**—Who will lead in what areas? What does equality look like for you two?

- **Children**—Are you both on the same page regarding when and how many children you'll have?
- **Faith**—What part does religion or spirituality play in your relationship?
- **Family Involvement**—What do both of your extended families expect from your relationship?
- **Worst-case scenarios**—How do you handle loss, crisis, faith changes, or career disruptions?
- **Future Planning**—Where do you see yourselves in five, ten, and fifteen years? Are you both still on the same trajectory?

Before you move on, you also must feel clear and confident in:

- The relationship's long-term viability.
- The relationship's PDF strength—Passion, Decision, and Friendship are present, tested, and satisfying.
- The alignment of strategic decisions.
- Each person's readiness to make a formal commitment.

This is your final evaluation Gate. If everything checks out, you don't need to think anymore.
It's time to decide.

## Gate Four: Engagement—Launch Agreement and Execution Mode

Exclusivity and a proposal mark the entrance to Gate Five. But it's more than just a ring; it's a launch agreement.
Brands do not launch a product nationwide unless the test market results are positive. They don't commit ad budgets and inventory until everything is locked. That's what this Gate represents.

Too many couples treat the proposal like a promise to figure things out later. They think engagement is when you start having hard conversations. That's a mistake.

If you've moved through the Test Market properly, there's nothing new to figure out. You're not hoping it works. You know it does.

In this phase, you're not making decisions—you're executing them. In Gate Five, you begin:

- Pre-marital counseling or coaching.
- Wedding planning.
- Finalizing logistics like housing, financial accounts, and legal prep.
- Coordinating agreed-upon geographic relocations.

You may move to Gate Five when the following have been completed:

- A formal proposal or declaration of commitment has been made and accepted.
- A wedding date has been set.
- All strategic questions have been answered.
- You have spent productive time in *execution mode*, focused on planning and preparing for launch.
- Both parties are emotionally, spiritually, and operationally ready to begin marriage.
- Both partners feel confident in the vision, logistics, and legacy of their future together.

This is not a casual devotion. It's a capital commitment. The moment you step into this phase, you're publicly accountable. Your brand is going live.

## Gate Five: Wedding: The Launch and Celebration of a Public Partnership

Consider this your grand opening. Your IPO. The confetti moment. A wedding is more than a party—it's a pivot. This shift in brand identity means the "I" becomes "we."

It's also a rare moment in time. Two sets of family and friend groups will be in the same room at the same time. This is when the people you love meet people they love. Your circles become one forever.

Don't rush through it.

- Feel the joy
- Let your communities bond
- Soak in the support that surrounds you
- Take the pictures
- Save the toasts

This day is a hinge. A launch. A gift. To move to the Co-Partnering Phase:

- Your marriage has been celebrated and launched
- Your community has witnessed and endorsed your bond
- You've begun your new life with joy and momentum

## Gate Six: Co-Partnering for Growth— The Strategy for Long-Term Marriage

No brand wants to be a one-hit wonder. Entrepreneurs dream of making a huge splash in their market, one that ripples for years and years. But consumer behaviors change, markets shift, and expectations rise. To stay in the game and create Brand Loyalty, businesses have to continually look for ways to improve. Your strategic relationship follows the same rules.

After you move past the honeymoon stage, it's vital to stay relevant to each other. You will face many seasons: babies, children, aging parents, illnesses, job changes, burnout, relocations, personal transformation, and more. You have to be intentional about making sure the relationship grows with you. This means continually adapting, evolving, and committing.

I know you're just thinking about dating now, so bookmark this page so you can come back to it after you launch because these are the strategies you'll want to implement when you come back from Tuscany.

- **Don't stop dating.** Schedule intentional connection points weekly, monthly, and annually.
- **Establish early rituals:** weekly check-ins, shared calendars, and joint financial planning.
- Use your USPs and DVPs to create a **Marriage Mission Statement** that clarifies your joint vision.
- **Host an annual "relationship review."** Celebrate your wins and diagnose issues.
- **Keep the PDF Triangle strong**—Light the fire of Passion often, make Decisions together, and deepen your Friendship.
- **Seek feedback** from mentors, counselors, coaches, and other successful couples.

Great brands never stop innovating, and neither do strong marriages. Great partnerships don't assume loyalty; they continually work for it and earn it. Love requires the same attention.

# The Six Launch Gates of True Love

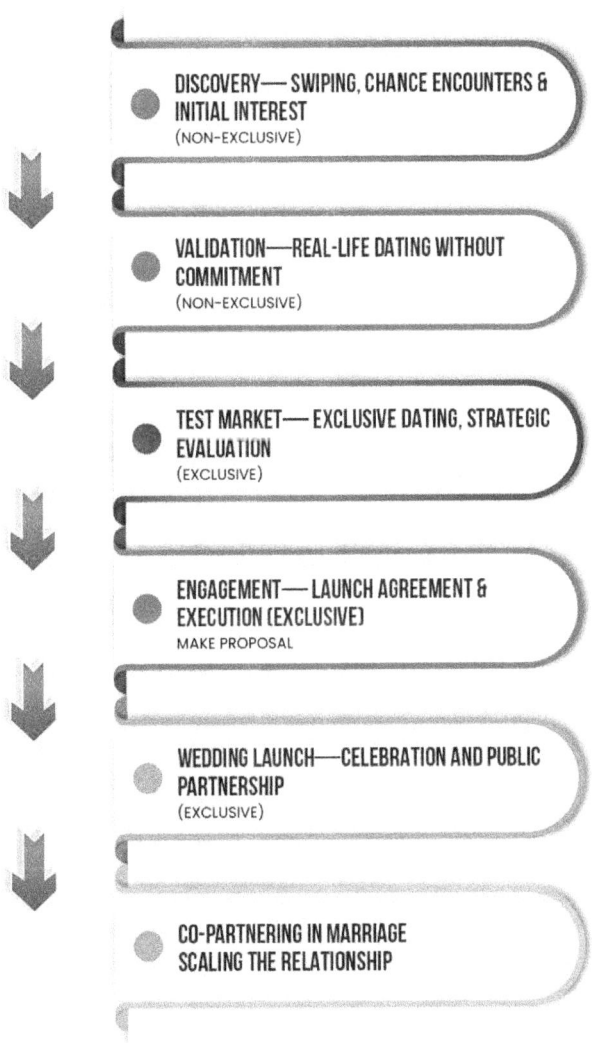

## Action Steps

The bullet points above will give you the basics of your action steps for this chapter. But to get started, determine which strategic Gate you are currently in and whether you're there on time or you've moved too fast into that period.

1. Which Gates have you passed?   1   2   3   4   5

2. Have you completed the recommended requirements to move past the previous Gate(s)? _____

3. If not, what will you do about it? (Check One)

   _____ Slow it down.
   _____ Find a coach to help me get back on track.
   _____ Break off the relationship and start dating strategically.

# CHAPTER EIGHTEEN

# Partnership Marketing in Marriage

*Marriage is not a noun; it's a verb.*
*It isn't something you get. It's something you do.*
*It's the way you love your partner every day.*

—Barbara De Angelis

As promised, I want to expand on the launch and post-launch of the relationship. I know, right now, marriage might seem like a long way off. However, the businesses that truly grow look far into the future. They begin planning for mergers and collaborations while they're writing their business proposals.

In branding, Partnership Marketing can be one of the most strategic decisions a business owner ever makes. When two strong brands, each with its own identity, come together to solve shared problems, amplify their message, and unlock growth neither could achieve alone, a powerful alliance is created. It's not about merging into one indistinct blur. It's about co-creating while preserving individuality.

That describes marriage—a long-term, high-stakes partner-marketing agreement. Two people aligned, not just emotionally but strategically, to build something lasting. Like partnership brands, couples learn to collaborate daily across campaigns, both mundane and extraordinary.

## Not a Big Bang

In the business world, every few years, someone labels a project "Big Bang." This code name signals some seismic initiative that will change everything—those of us who have been around for a while chuckle behind closed doors. Big Bangs rarely work. Bloated with expectations and often out of touch with day-to-day realities, they seldom live up to the hype.

What actually moves the needle in marketing? The consistent, sometimes boring, relentless execution of small things.

Love works the same way. Hollywood and pop culture try their best to sell us the Big Bang version of romance—fireworks, a dramatic proposal, and the wedding day as the crowning moment. But in *The Love Prescription*, John and Julie Schwarz Gottman remind us that love isn't created in bursts. It's built through habits. The prescription for real love isn't a booster shot; it's a daily vitamin—small, intentional acts done every day, not just on anniversaries and holidays.

## Love Is a Language

That's where *The 5 Love Languages* by Gary Chapman becomes essential. Dr. Chapman presents more than a gimmick; he shares a user manual for communicating love to your "partner brand" (as well as your children). He believes that each person receives and gives love in different ways. Just like some only speak Italian and others need to hear your voice in Spanish, we best understand love when our partner speaks in our native tongue.

As the title suggests, Dr. Chapman defines five love languages:

- **Words of Affirmation.** I like to think of these as good PR. Encouragement and appreciation—any kind of verbal recognition—deliver a message that reinforces brand loyalty.
- **Acts of Service** could be compared to operational support. When we fix the sink, take the dog for a walk, and do the dishes, we say, "I love you." It's logistics in motion, and it speaks volumes.
- **Gifts** might remind us of seasonal promotions. The value isn't in how much it costs but rather in the symbolism and effort of the offering. Thoughtful tokens that are memorable and evoke emotion are brand-reinforcing.
- **Quality Time** falls in the category of exclusive access. It's more than being in the same room; it's being *present*. It's a one-to-one brand experience, curated and undistracted.
- **Physical Touch** is sensory branding. It can be as simple as a kiss, a hug, or a hand on the back as you pass by. These nonverbal cues build emotional memory, just like great packaging or a tactile retail display.

If you don't know your partner's primary love language, you're likely delivering value in the wrong format. Imagine trying to sell a premium skincare line to someone looking for toothpaste. You may be putting in effort, but it's misaligned. Partner marketing fails when brands misunderstand each other's consumers.

## More Partnership Strategies

Your marriage needs to be like a high-end Customer Relationship Management (CRM) system; however, you have only one customer who matters. Businesses get a CRM to manage and improve the way they interact with their clients. The CRM tracks important dates, preferences, previous orders, and more. It allows the company to send the message that the things that are important to the customer are important to the business, and it does everything in its power to help the customer feel loved and valued.

And just like in business, you don't earn loyalty through launch events—a wedding. A long-lasting business relationship, like a marriage, evolves through reliable delivery, personalized experience, and active listening.

Partnership Marketing also means shared campaigns. Whether it's parenting, planning for a move, tackling debt, or just deciding what's for dinner, these integrated marketing systems need teamwork. A successful partnership negotiates roles, allocates resources, and evaluates outcomes. The brands that thrive in co-marketing don't compete for the spotlight; they stay aligned on the mission.

And don't forget about re-engagement strategies. Every long-term relationship goes through seasons of stagnation. Smart brands reintroduce themselves from time to time. They run new campaigns that surprise and delight.

Great marriages use the same strategy. You can reignite your relationship by planning a spontaneous weekend trip or leaving a note on the mirror. A new shared ritual can strengthen the bond and create new excitement. Don't consider these relationship-building events as luxuries. Think of them as strategies to maintain long-term emotional connection. The marriage flame doesn't have to die, but it will need to be rekindled every now and again.

If you believe the myth that love magically happens and then sustains itself, you'll fail. The truth? Love, like brand equity, erodes if left unattended. To Date Like a Brand, we have to stop chasing the Big Bang and start building brand equity. It's time to tend the fire and show up for the little things. We must shift our mindset. You have more than a spouse. You have a partner and co-creator, a co-CEO, and a lifelong collaborator in the most important brand you'll ever build: the story of us.

## Micro-Moments That Build Macro Love

Fortunately, you don't have to leave love to chance. That also means you can't use a *Field of Dreams* philosophy for your marriage any more than an entrepreneur can think, "If I build it, they will come." Day by day, we have to do at least one thing to build our brand. These don't have to be grand gestures. Small, high-return "marketing actions" will keep your marriage healthy, engaged, and emotionally resonant.

For instance, simply discovering and speaking the love language your partner understands can be powerful. And just like hearing the words "I love you" in Italian can make you feel tingly, even those occasional gestures in another love language can build your Love For Your Life.

- **Words of Affirmation** invite you to say one encouraging thing each day. You could start with one of these:

    - "I'm proud of how you handled that today."
    - "You look great this morning."
    - "I love the way you think."

- **Acts of Service** will do at least one helpful act without being asked. Consider any of these:

    - Make the bed.
    - Pick up their favorite snack.
    - Handle a task they dislike.

- **Quality Time** creates a moment of undivided attention. For instance:

    - A ten-minute conversation without phones.
    - Sitting together with coffee before work.
    - A short evening walk.

- **Gifts** will offer a small surprise. Something like these:

    - A sticky note on the mirror.
    - Their favorite treat.
    - A meaningful song or article you came across.

- **Physical Touch** will be intentional with one of these ideas to get you started:

    - A hug longer than ten seconds.
    - A hand on the back, shoulder, or thigh.
    - Cuddle without distraction, even briefly.

In addition to Dr. Chapman's Love Languages, you could also start the day with a simple question: "How can I make today easier for you?" Proactive brands always move forward more effectively than reactive ones. Fixing a problem after it occurs is appreciated, but intentionally taking care of the issue so it doesn't happen adds value to the relationship.

You also need an evening routine, a way to connect at the end of the day. Consider a short check-in before bed: "What was the best part of your day?" Little things like touching feet under the covers or whispering, "I'm glad I get to do life with you," make a world of difference.

Love isn't a performance; it's practice. Every small act is an investment—grabbing her hand when walking to the car, leaving a note on his windshield, opening doors for her, or fixing him a cup of coffee or glass of wine in the evening. Though they require so little effort, they add to your brand value. And in this marketing campaign, you're not just building a marriage. You're building a brand that people, including your kids, friends, and community, will remember for its quiet strength and everyday beauty.

In marketing, one of the most strategic decisions a brand can make is to enter a partner marketing alliance. When two strong brands, each with their own identity, come together to solve shared problems, amplify their message, and unlock growth neither could achieve alone, the return is exponential.

Marriage has the potential to be the most magnificent long-term, high-stakes Partnership Marketing agreement known to humanity. Perhaps you've seen it and wondered how they did it. That couple who just celebrated fifty years and still look at each other like they're dating—they invested in Partnership Marketing. They might not have even realized what they did, but I guarantee you, they worked hard, and they worked together.

When two people in alignment, not just emotionally but strategically, work to build something that lasts and collaborate daily to navigate the mundane and celebrate the extraordinary, something grand is created. It takes a mindset on Partnership Marketing to achieve your true Love For Your Life.

## Action Steps

You've just read an entire chapter of action steps, ones that must be practiced every day for your entire marriage. When you're still in the Purpose part of the 6 Ps Platform, looking forward to Partnership Marketing can spur two more questions: Do I want to invest my energy and time into showing love and being intentional with my actions toward this person for the next seventy years? Is the person I'm dating willing to do what it takes to be a partner at this level?

# CHAPTER NINETEEN

# The Annual Relationship Review

*Perfection is not attainable,
but if we chase perfection we can catch excellence.*
—Vince Lombardi

*The main thing is to keep the main thing the main thing.*
—Stephen Covey

Performance reviews are essential. If you want to excel, you have to compare your current status to where you were. We don't think twice about running performance reviews for our jobs and our finances. Many review their fitness levels on a regular basis, and if you're avoiding waste, you even review your streaming subscriptions at least once a year. Still, most people neglect to audit what is arguably your most important status—your love life.

Whether you're dating, committed, or married, one ritual separates brands that grow from those that stagnate: the annual review. Great brands don't assume loyalty—they earn it, year after year, by re-evaluating their strategy, optimizing their value proposition, and listening to their audience.

Your love life deserves the same treatment.

The *Date Like a Brand* framework gives you two powerful tools: the DVP (Dating Value Proposition) and the PDF (Passion, Decision, Friendship) models. Taking time to intentionally reflect on both at least annually will prove invaluable. If you're single, you'll want to review your own DVP as well as the DVP of those you're dating. Plus, consider the PDF of each potential relationship. If you're in a committed relationship, review the models on your own and then together.

## Part I: Reassessing Your Dating Value Proposition

Whether you're actively dating or not, your DVP is continually evolving. Ask yourself a few questions to determine how your current DVP stacks up against your DVP of a year ago:

- **Mind**: Did I grow intellectually this year? Am I curious, communicative, and emotionally intelligent?
- **Body**: Do I prioritize my health and hygiene? Have I been managing a healthy weight? How is my level of sexual confidence?
- **Soul**: Do my actions align with my values? Do I bring joy, peace, and purpose to myself? To a partner?
- **Resources**: Am I building a stable foundation—financial, professional, or otherwise?

Be honest with yourself. Where did you move forward this year? Did you regress in any area? Do any areas need a strategic push?

# The Annual Relationship Review

If your DVP isn't growing, don't be surprised if your dating results stall, too. This isn't about chasing perfection—it's about momentum. Like any product in the marketplace, stagnation breeds irrelevance.

## Part II: Taking the Temperature of the Relationship by Evaluating the Passion, Friendship, and Decision

If you're in a committed relationship, this is where the real brand work happens. Just like brand managers review customer loyalty metrics, you and your partner should review your relationship's health across three key pillars:

- **Passion**: Is there still a spark? Do we desire one another physically and emotionally?
- **Decision**: Are we both still choosing each other—actively and consciously?
- **Friendship**: Are we laughing, talking, and sharing life as true companions?

Bring out the PDF Scorecard, and implement the most important step: discussion. Where are we strong? Where are we drifting? What do we want to improve? Have the courage to ask, "What needs to evolve for us to keep thriving together?"

## Set Annual Goals—Together or Solo

You wouldn't launch a new product without a roadmap. So don't exit your review without a plan.

- If you're single, define how you'll upgrade your DVP this year.

  - What new habits would you like to create?
  - Do you need a mindset shift?
  - Would your life benefit from therapy or relocation?
  - Should you take a pause from dating to reinvest in yourself?

- If you're in a relationship—dating or married—commit to strengthening your PDF profile. You might consider one or more of these:

  - A weekly check-in.
  - Couples therapy.
  - More and intentional intimacy.
  - Rekindling shared hobbies.

Whatever you decide, be sure to write it down, revisit it often, and treat it like a performance pact—with yourself or your significant other.

## **Take Action**

Make a date with yourself or your partner. You might choose New Year's Day, your birthday, your anniversary, or even tax season if that's your vibe. What matters is consistency.

You are your own brand. Your relationship is your most important co-branding exercise. Both deserve a strategy session.

So make it annual. Make it honest. Make it count.

# CHAPTER TWENTY

# The Circle of Love For Life

*In the circle of life, it's the wheel of fortune.*
—The Lion King

By now, you realize *Dating Like a Brand* goes way beyond how to find a match, impress someone, and "optimize" your love life. Sure, it's a book about dating, but I wanted it to be more than just your typical dating advice book. You see, I want you to find love—the real kind.

Love is so much bigger than a fleeting emotion that comes and goes with a mood or a bad day. I have experienced that deeper, fuller, richer love, and I want that for you, too. True love builds lives, not just relationships. It does more than simply entertain; it provides healing. As Stevie Wonder so wisely sang, "Love's in need of love today." And in a time when we have more options but fewer commitments and more choices but less clarity than ever before, this message couldn't be more urgent.

The world is overwhelmed by swipes, lists, DMs, and situationships. Optimists might boast about the dropping divorce rates. But perhaps the encouraging number only reflects the fact that marriage rates have hit an all-time low.[18] Confusion, disillusionment, and discouragement rule the dating landscape because, although we have the tools to connect, we've lost the foundation on which to build.

All this, and the fact that you needed a book to help jumpstart your dating life, just emphasizes the demand for a new system. The 6 Ps Platform, which includes **Pre-Assessment, Purpose, Positioning, Prime Prospecting, Performance Dating,** and **Partnership Marketing,** invites you to approach dating like a brand.

Successful Brands don't operate by chance. They constantly look for clarity. They know their target, set clear objectives, and deliver measurable output. Those markers evaluate every campaign, launch, and lifecycle phase of the brand.

In each of the four phases, you should name three specific markers to determine whether you're on the right track in your dating life.

- **Target**—Who is the focus of this phase of love?
- **Objective**—What will you learn or do in the phase of love?
- **Output**—What result will this phase of love create?

These brand life phases are vital as marketers judge how far their campaign has traveled. So, let's look at your life through the brand strategist's lens with the Circle of Love for Life[IP].

## Phase One of the Circle of Love For Life: Love of Self

- **Target of Love**: You
- **Objective**: To grow from selfishness into self-love through knowledge, care, respect, and responsibility

- **Output**: A whole, growing, and steadily developing of **Mind, Body, Soul,** and **Resources**. This phase will move a person from "I exist" to "I'm becoming"

You begin life entirely dependent. You cry to survive, demand to be cared for, and are unable to distinguish yourself from the world around you. That isn't bad; it's by design. You were made to be selfish in the beginning. That instinct kept you alive.

As you grew, the target of your love transformed to include a less selfish, more intentional lifestyle. You learned to **know** yourself, **care** for yourself, **respect** yourself, and **take responsibility** for yourself. Do you remember those four identifiers of true love? Every time you look within, you form a specific identity and move from self-preservation to self-possession. After you develop and understand the foundation of who you are deep inside, it's time to move to Phase Two.

## Phase Two of the Circle of Love For Life: Love of Source

- **Target of Love:** Your Source (God, Truth, or Meaning)
- **Objective:** To align with a higher truth and live with purpose, especially in Soul
- **Output:** Amplified personal growth anchored in values and expressed through Mind, Body, Soul, and Resources

As your identity forms, you ask a deeper question: What is all this for? You also seek the source of your existence—a truth bigger than yourself. Many look to God, others find it in a spiritual philosophy or life principle. Regardless, your source of life is something that transcends you. Because the target of your love shifts from self to source, you find yourself wanting to know that source, caring about your alignment with it, respecting its truth, and taking responsibility for living in the truth of the source.

Your growth has become purposeful because you're learning to live harmoniously with your values and higher calling. The output is intentional and value-driven growth with particular depth in your soul because that's where integrity lives.

## Phase Three in the Circle of Love For Life: Love of Mate

- **Target of Love:** Your Partner
- **Objective:** To co-create connection, commitment, and synergy in love
- **Output:** A life built together—enhanced growth in **Mind, Body, Soul,** and **Resources** through partnership

Now that you've laid a strong foundation and your alignment is clear, you're ready for relational love. Previously, your love came from a place of neediness, but now it pours from a place of abundance. You can truly love someone with whom you are equally yoked, similarly grounded, and ready to build with. With an expanded capacity for love, you can extend your love of self and source to know your mate deeply, care for them selflessly, respect their individuality, and take responsibility for their well-being in addition to yours. You now have the ability to grow with another person in ways you could never grow alone. The output is a relationship where both individuals flourish, co-powered by love and alignment.

## Phase Four of the Circle of Love For Life: Love of Legacy

- **Target of Love:** Your legacy—your own children or others.
- **Objective:** To pass on love, wisdom, and security to the next generation
- **Output:** A life launched with a head start. A young person equipped with identity and stability in **Mind, Body, Soul,** and **Resources**

Everyone wants to leave a legacy. You can bestow nothing greater on the next generation than the ability to move through the Lifecycle of Love as easily as possible. Some will choose to have children and give them a jumpstart on their love journey. But even if you never have an offspring of your own, the possibility to leave a legacy of love abounds.

The foster system needs volunteers and those willing to adopt. Organizations created to build up children and teens look for mentors, and every local sports program needs coaches, assistant coaches, and volunteers to maintain the fields and work the concession stands. If you're a person of faith, your church, synagogue, or mosque is probably full of kids who could use an extra adult to help them navigate life.

Whatever way you decide to put your love into action, love now turns outward in an even bigger capacity than with your mate. A mate will co-create and develop synergy with you, but young people—until they move to at least Phase Two or Three of the Lifecycle of Love—will not have the capacity to reciprocate like an adult who has walked through these phases.

You will give what you once needed:

- **Knowledge** of self and the one who needs love

- **Care** that protects
- **Respect** that empowers
- **Responsibility** that prepares the target to become the next ripple in the pond

This Phase of the Circle uses everything you've learned to give the next generation a head start on understanding real love. They will be able to move through Phase One surrounded by security and identity, and you'll be able to lay the foundation for them to develop their own Mind, Body, Soul, and Resources with confidence. This Legacy Phase is what makes it a circle. When you train the next generation, it continues.

# The Circle of Love For Life

Here's the process condensed into a table so you can access it quickly:

## Circle of Love For Life—Target, Objective, and Output

| Phase | Target of Love | Objective | Output |
|---|---|---|---|
| **ONE: Love of Self** | You | Grow from selfishness into self-love through knowledge, care, respect, and responsibility | A whole and growing person—developed in the Four Pillars |
| **TWO: Love of Source** | Your Source (God, Truth, Meaning) | Align with a higher truth and live with purpose, especially in the soul | Amplified personal growth—anchored in values and expressed through all dimensions |
| **THREE: Love of Mate** | Your Partner | Co-create connection, commitment, and synergy in love | Enhanced growth through partnership and development of the Four Pillars |
| **FOUR: Love of Legacy** | Your Child or Legacy | Pass on love, wisdom, and security to the next generation | A young life equipped with identity, stability, and purpose |

## Take Action

By applying marketing tactics to your life, you can become more intentional with your time and energy. Like any great brand, you are built to fulfill your purpose (to love) and deliver lasting value (growth in Mind, Body, Soul, and Resources). It will take time and effort, but I believe in you.

1. When you look at the Phases of the Lifecycle of Love, where are you today?

   _____
   _____
   _____

2. Who or what is your source? What is the catalyst for your life?

   _____
   _____
   _____

3. Take a minute and look forward. What will life look like when you have a mate to be the target of your love? What will be your personal objective in that phase?

   _____
   _____
   _____
   _____
   _____
   _____

4. Again, looking forward, how will you leave a legacy? Even if you never have a mate, you can pass on love to a child.

   What age group do you relate to most?

   _____
   _____
   _____

   How will you use your talents or passions to show a child or teen what it means to love without fear of abuse or unrealistic expectations?

   _____
   _____
   _____

Whether you're launching your love life, rebuilding after heartbreak, or passing love on to the next generation

**Date like a brand.**
**Love like a legacy.**
**And build like it matters.**
*Because it does.*

# BONUS CHAPTER

# How It All Began—"The Vinnifer Story"

*Every love story is beautiful, but ours is my favorite.*
—Anonymous

Maybe you're wondering, *Does this work in real life, or does Vince just see marketing strategies everywhere?* Truthfully, I wrote this book because I lived it. The *Date Like a Brand* framework and strategy are more than a theory. They have been road-tested, and they work.

Love feels so unpredictable, and to some extent, it always will be. Life is unpredictable. It's full of delays and detours. But like with any road, if you know what to look for and learn from others' wrong turns, you can avoid the most significant obstacles and roadblocks. This structure gives you a navigational system that brings clarity to the chaos.

So, to give you an idea of how this framework can play out in your own life, I'd like to share my story. From Discovering my DVP and PDF to Launch and Loyalty, I've walked through every stage and phase and seen the power of every step. In fact, the reason I felt compelled to put it on paper is the number of people I've seen implement this process and find success.

Welcome to the world of Vince and Jennifer Hudson—AKA Vinnifer. (Yes, this is our version of "Bennifer"—Ben Affleck and Jennifer Lopez—with a bit less drama and publicity.)

## Discovering My Own DVP and PDF

Perhaps it's the natural marketing instincts inside me or the foundation my parents laid out for me, but even before I understood the need for a DVP, I knew I didn't want to date aimlessly. I remember when I was nineteen, I told someone, "I'm not getting married until I turn twenty-five." I always dated with intention.

My parents shaped my view immensely. We didn't have an abundance of Resources, but we always had enough. I learned early not to want much but to strive for everything. They gave me a worldview that allowed me to recognize value beyond status, and this value-based life spilled into my dating philosophy early.

I understood the profile of my DVP early in the game. I was always skinny and just a bit above average in looks (my smile was my best feature), so I was building from a solid "6" on body with my target audience in the neighborhood. My parents were teachers, which provided a solid life but no trust fund, so resources were up to me. Luckily, being raised in the Bible Belt by two educators who modeled character, consistency, and curiosity gave me a strong connection to faith and learning. Early on, I realized I was predisposed to a high Mind and Soul score, so I needed to develop those as high as possible.

## How It All Began—"The Vinnifer Story"

Now, as far as the DVP I was seeking—Body probably topped my list (as with most teens), but Mind held a close second. I knew I'd run in circles where that would be important, and it would be key to meeting my goals for children who prioritized education. Those were the primary values I carried as a standard into the dating world.

Along the way, I met many women I gave a true "Probably Would Marry" rating, but so few ever crossed into the "Definitely Would Marry" category. The more I learned about relationships, the more I understood that the reason so few moved into that top category was that our PDFs didn't align.

Some relationships would have strong Passion and Friendship, but one of us just couldn't Decide. Other times, the Decision was easy because it felt like a safe choice, but Friendship or Passion just didn't feel right. Getting to all three at a sufficient and sustainable level eluded me in every relationship.

Until I met Jennifer . . .

## Discovery: One Night in New Orleans

I loved visiting New Orleans during the Essence Music Festival. One night as I walked out of a Festival party, I saw a girl sitting alone on the steps outside the hotel ballroom. Her elegance and radiance immediately struck me. Plus, she looked totally unbothered, a trait I didn't see often in a girl sitting alone outside a social gathering. Something about her caught me off guard. It was more than just her looks. A part of me knew I needed to meet her.

I changed course to walk toward her, and after I introduced myself, I asked if I could sit. She said yes, and we talked at length. I enjoyed the ease of the conversation, and grace spilled out of her. My System 1 brain could feel the chemistry. We took a picture together—pre-iPhone era—and I asked where she was staying. (No, not to follow her. I wanted to know which front desk to call.)

The next day, I called and invited her to a lunch event my company was sponsoring. We spent a good part of the afternoon talking and connecting. When I got back to my room, I called my best friend, described her and our respective "chip count," and said, "I think I met the girl I'm going to marry." To which he responded, "You're probably going to have to work for this one."

He was right.

## The Validation Period

Talk about validation! We both had to invest in this long-distance dating. Minutes in that age weren't unlimited; those everyday phone calls came with a price tag. I flew to see her. She flew to see me.

I guess we needed to take the conversation just a bit further because my thirty-year-old self assumed she was twenty-five. She was actually twenty-three. Two years might not seem like much, but in terms of life stage, it mattered. But even after we recognized the difference, we pressed on.

I encouraged her to apply for a role at Procter & Gamble, and she landed it—no easy feat—but her "mind" had already passed my interview. This brought her to Cincinnati, and for the first time in our relationship, we were in the same city. I was ready to move into Capital Commitment (put a ring on it). But while we had a big Friendship and good Passion, the Decision on her end wasn't there. And for tremendous collaboration success, both brands have to be ready to launch.

# How It All Began—"The Vinnifer Story"

## The Breakup

You might not be expecting this segment in a story about dating success, but it's true. The new job, new city, and new expectations sent Jennifer into her Quarter-Life Crisis. Plus, her avoidant attachment style began to surface. The rapid changes overwhelmed her.

She returned the keys to my house and car and said with deep sincerity, "I'm just not ready."

I responded with the hardest truth I'd ever spoken. "I suggest we take a four-year break. You should go date other people, and I will, too."

That moment marked a pivotal shift for both of us. We re-entered the Discovery phase—not together, but apart. It gave us both time to mature and develop.

## Separate Paths, Parallel Growth

Our lives went in different directions over the next several years. We stayed in touch—not romantically, but respectfully. I transferred to Seattle, and she stayed in Cincinnati. I dated other women (well, many other women), and she (wait for it . . . ) got engaged..

Eventually, her avoidant attachment and hesitancy to decide clashed with the intensity of her younger fiancé, and she broke off the engagement. She told me it moved too fast and did not feel their connection (PDF) was strong enough to warrant a forever commitment. We both continued to mature and date other people, but we maintained our friendship, and the idea of a relationship relaunch lived in the back of both our minds.

## Test Market 2.0—The Comeback

And this is where I discovered a key insight to the *Date Like a Brand* model. "Targeting Lapsed users" is a viable, often necessary strategy. It's important to remember: Sometimes the product isn't the problem. The market conditions just aren't right. And the only way to know is to let time pass, growth happen, and clarity return.

Whether you'd like to call it fate or a product of faith, four years later, after we'd both given up on the relationship, we both got assigned to work on the COVERGIRL® "Lash Blast" launch. We worked together. Won awards. Rekindled something—not just emotionally, but relationally.

Four years after we decided we should both date other people, we reconnected with clarity. Our respective DVPs were even stronger. Our PDF triangle was whole. Our Decision was mutual.

## Enter Pre-Launch and Launch

I took her back to New Orleans, the place we met, to ask her to marry me. This time, we both knew what we were choosing. There wasn't any hype, just history, honesty, and hard-won clarity. Our story might not sound like a fairy tale, but it is the story of a two growing brands—a tale of depth, data, and decisive love.

We officially and ceremoniously launched on March 13th, when Jennifer Holiday (not the Tony Award-winning star of the stage production of *Dream Girls*) became Jennifer Hudson (not the Academy Award-winning star of the onscreen version of the same show), and the real work began.

How It All Began—"The Vinnifer Story"

## Loyalty: Building Real Life Together

Life has been full since we launched. Because we both waited to marry until we were pretty ripe in our life cycle, we wasted no time starting our line extensions, which we repeated every two years. Olivia, Ava, and Vanna. (Yes, all the Vs in each name were an intentional branding device.)

Ava arrived during one of our more stressful times. I had taken an international assignment in Singapore. A young family in a new culture and country can test a relationship. It definitely stretched us, but we'd set ourselves up for success by making sure we were aligned before we launched. This allowed us to adapt, grow, and become anchored.

Another move to New Jersey when I started working with Samsung® pushed the boundaries of our relationship again. And while we are both every bit as grateful for the arrival of Vanna as we were for our first two beautiful girls, every added family member means an adaptation in the relationship.

I believe I was always meant to be a girl dad. I grew up admiring my sister, Mona, and the relationship she had with our dad. Now, over fifteen years later, Jennifer and I continue to sacrifice and invest energy in our family. But the reward is priceless. We have a strong relationship and three wonderful daughters developing their own individual brands.

## Write Your Own Story

The story Jennifer and I share isn't just a personal victory. It's validation. The *Date Like a Brand* model helped me navigate every stage of love. It gave me the courage to know when to push forward and when to walk away. It developed my understanding of what to value, how to think, where to wait, and when to choose.

Recently, as I've honed the *Date Like a Brand* philosophy, Jennifer and I did our own DVP Market Chips Game. We took ourselves back to when we were dating and individually rated ourselves. We weren't surprised to discover our overall Dating Chip Score matched. At the same time, we each brought different strengths to balance each other and our household vision. We're living proof that knowing your own DVP and finding someone who is a good complement significantly increases marriage success.

More importantly, I've loved watching this model work with my friends. Over the years, as I coached people through their own dating decisions—men and women alike—I've seen this framework be effective over and over again.

I hope you've come to see this is more than just a theory. *Date Like a Brand* is a framework for clarity in the chaos of modern love.

I may not have all the answers. But I believe I found a better way to ask the right questions. This model didn't create love, but it did allow me to see it, understand it, return to it, and commit to it.

And now, it's yours.

I pray it helps you find, retarget, or simply grow the kind of love that's worth launching and keeping. I want this framework to give you the tools to write your own love story—one that you can tell your children and grandchildren to help them learn how to successfully Date Like a Brand.

## A Change, A Movement—Learn More

As a marketer, my job has always been to change the way people see things because, as Wayne Dyer said, "When you change the way you look at things, the things you look at change." My hope is that your love journey changes because you've changed how you look at it.

## How It All Began—"The Vinnifer Story"

From now on, when someone says "I love you," it should land differently because you now unpack the evidence of love (all four). When you see a couple walking by, you'll instinctively decode which of the four DVP elements each of them was solving for (even if they don't consciously know it themselves). Most importantly, I hope it changes the way you look in the mirror: How will I grow my Mind, Body, Soul, and Resources this week?

As you navigate this V.U.C.A. dating game, you'll carry an evolved screener (or swiper) not just for who you're choosing but for the quality of your potential: Passion, Decision, and Friendship together. With each step in relationships (forward or backward), you'll at least know which Gate you're in and what it truly takes to move to the next one.

Ultimately, that's the goal of this book: to change the way you look at love so that love itself can change. And so that you can write your own love story as your own Brand Manager.

Start now. Join the movement.

What if the key frameworks in this book were brought to life in an app—customized just for you—with the latest in AI tech guiding you through actual use of these frameworks and my perspective always on, always updated, and coaching you in real-time situations? That's exactly what the Date Like a Brand AI Coaching App is built to do.

Visit DateLikeABrand.com to take the next step.

# ACKNOWLEDGMENTS

In sequential order

First, thanks to God, the originator of all things, including love. Thanks to my Brand Creators, my parents, who launched two line extensions (my sister and me) into a home filled with abundant love. You taught us by example to give more than we take, so this book has the intent of giving some of that love to others. I also want to thank the other half of that "us," my sister, Mona, who embodies a loving soul that gives so much to so many and is the best friend/sister combo a guy could ever ask for.

To not just my better half, but my better 95 percent, my wife, Jennifer Hudson (not "the" Jennifer Hudson, but we do have a funny story about meeting the amazing celebrity at a fundraiser). Thank you for actually walking this winding, but worth it, road with me as soulmate, friend, parent, and fellow marketer. Without you holding down the fort while I took a break to write the book, it wouldn't have been possible.

To all my female co-workers over the decades who let me play "Love Coach" and give dating advice without a license. I won't name names as the list would be too long or have unintentional omissions, but this book stems from the many situations that we laughed (and cried) about.

Thanks, too, to my ad agency friends who sat with me, filling out spreadsheets about their exes when we had downtime at commercial shoots—fun times!

And finally, to my many marketing comrades/bosses/mentors at Procter and Gamble who made me a sharper Brand Person as I developed this concept: Kirk Perry, MaryLynn Ferguson McHugh, Joe Arcuri, Pat Conklin, Dan Epstein, Jim Stengel, Marc Pritchard, Paul Alexander, and of course, Esi Eggleston-Bracey. Also, thanks to all the brands, bosses, and teams after P&G for allowing me to grow and contribute.

P.S. While he may not remember this, my in-person quick meeting with Steve Harvey (author of the must-read "consumer understanding" book, *Think Like a Man, Act Like a Lady*) was a critical part of my inspiration to write this book.

# ENDNOTES

1. Yau, Nathan. *Flowing Data.* "Shifts in How Couples Meet, Online Takes the Top." Accessed January 20, 2025. https://flowingdata.com/2019/03/15/shifts-in-how-couples-meet-online-takes-the-top-spot/
2. Volpe, Allie. *Vox.* "The Surprising Truth about Loneliness." August 13, 2024. https://www.vox.com/even-better/366620/loneliness-epidemic-coping-demographics-america-social-connection-mental-health.
3. Gellen, Larry. *New York Post.* "The Fascinating History of How Courtship Became Dating." May 15, 2016. https://nypost.com/2016/05/15/the-fascinating-history-of-how-courtship-became-dating/.
4. Avery, Charlotte. *Achology.com.* "Unraveling the Mind: An Exploration of Howard Gardner's Nine Types of Intelligence. Access January 25, 2025. https://achology.com/psychology/exploration-of-dr-howard-gardners-nine-types-of-intelligence/.
5. Hollander, Anne. *New York Times.* "When Fat Was in Fashion." October 23, 1977. https://www.nytimes.com/1977/10/23/archives/when-fat-was-in-fashion-abundant-flesh-was-a-thing-of-beauty-to.html
6. Cooper, Audrey; Hammond, Katie; Koliadko, Eden; Shoemake, John; Young, Emily; et al. *Journal of Interdisciplinary Undergraduate Research, Volume 2, Article 2.* "Self-Rated Physical Attractiveness, Attractiveness Standards, and Expectation Deviations in Romantic

Partners Among Non-Married University Students" 2010. https://knowledge.e.southern.edu/cgi/viewcontent.cgi?article=1011&context=jiur.

7   Ibid.

8   Footnote:Cooper, Audrey; Hammond, Katie; Koliadko, Eden; Shoemaker, John; Young, Emily; and Ysseldyke, Lauren "Self-Rated Physical Attractiveness, Attractiveness Standards, and Expectation Deviations in Romantic Partners Among Non-Married University Students." *Journal of Interdisciplinary Undergraduate Research.* Vol. 2, Article 2. 2010.

9   *Jimenez Law Firm.* "What Percentage of Marriages End in Divorce Because of Money?" December 29, 2022. https://www.thejimenezlawfirm.com/what-percent-of-marriages-end-in-divorce-because-of-money/

10  *John Hopkins Medical.* "Forgiveness: Your Health Depends on it." Accessed February 8, 2025. https://www.hopkinsmedicine.org/health/wellness-and-prevention/forgiveness-your-health-depends-on-it

11  Mayo Clinic Staff. *Mayo Clinic.* "Forgiveness: Letting Go of Grudges and Bitterness." November 22, 2022. https://www.mayoclinic.org/healthy-lifestyle/adult-health/in-depth/forgiveness/art-20047692.

12  Robinson, Lawrence and Smith, Melinda, M.A. *HelpGuide.org.* "Surviving Tough Times by Building Resilience." Accessed February 8, 2025. https://www.helpguide.org/mental-health/stress/surviving-tough-times.

13  *VC Star.* "Healing Power of Meditation and Prayer." June 6, 2012. https://www.vcstar.com/story/life/blogs/vc-style/2012/06/06/healing_power_of_meditation_prayer/89120270/.

14  Sternberg, R. J. *Psychological Review* "A Triangular Theory of Love." 1986. 93(2), 119–135.

# Endnotes

15 *EducationPolicy*. "Higher Education Enrollment Trends by Gender, 1970 to 2025." March 20, 2019. https://educationalpolicy.org/hello-world/.
16 *U.S. Bureau of Labor Statistics*. "TED: The Economics Daily." January 10, 2007. https://www.bls.gov/opub/ted/2007/jan/wk2/art03.htm.
17 *Congress.gov*. "Real Wage Trends, 1979-2019." December 28, 2020. https://www.congress.gov/crs-product/R45090.
18 *Wilkinson and FinkBeiner*. "Divorce Statistics: Over 115 Studies, Facts and Rates for 2024." Accessed April 16, 2025. https://www.wf-lawyers.com/divorce-statistics-and-facts.

# ABOUT THE AUTHOR

Vince Hudson, Fortune 500 C-Suite marketer, is also a seasoned architect of brand success with a thirty-year track record at industry giants like Procter & Gamble, AMEX, Samsung, and Meta. Vince has spent the last thirty years honing his understanding of what makes relationships thrive, personally navigating the journey from dating to marriage and fatherhood. A proud HBCU graduate, Vince calls himself the Chief Marketing Officer of Love and serves on the Board of Trustees for Dillard University and resides in North Bergen County with his wife, Jennifer, and their daughters, Olivia, Ava, and Vanna.

Connect with Vince at Vince@Datelikeabrand.com

# BRING VINCE HUDSON TO YOUR NEXT EVENT!

- Building Your Personal Brand: Learn to maximize your life's potential using proven branding strategies tailored for today's dynamic environment.

- Dating with Strategic Intent: Discover how to effectively and efficiently leverage powerful branding concepts to revolutionize your dating life.

- Expertise You Can Trust: Vince brings over 30 year of corporate experience on some of the world's biggest brands, combined with an equally long passion for studying and living love and relationships.

Book Vince for your event today at:
## DateLikeABrand.com

# Join the Date Like a Brand Movement!

♥ ♥ ♥ ♥ ♥ ♥ ♥

Join a community dedicated to revolutionizing love and relationships through powerful branding principles.

- <u>Free Exercises</u>: Practical activities to deepen your understanding and enhance your dating success.

- <u>DLAB "AI Coach" App</u>: Your personal end-to-end dating coach, always accessible from your pocket.

- <u>Fresh Insights & Discussions</u>: Stay engaged with regularly updated content and interactive conversations.

Start Exploring Today At: DateLikeABrand.com

# Elevate Your Dating Experience with the DATE LIKE A BRAND "AI-COACH" APP:

♥ ♥ ♥ ♥ ♥ ♥ ♥

- Dive deep into personalized exercises to build your brand

- Honestly assess where you stand in your relationships—past and present

- Get real-time, AI-driven advice tailored to your unique situation (or situationship!)

Download the app today at: DateLikeABrand.com

# CONNECT WITH VINCE

Follow Vince on your favorite social platforms and unlock the potential of your brand in love and relationships.

# DateLikeABrand.com

# THIS BOOK IS PROTECTED INTELLECTUAL PROPERTY

The author of this book values Intellectual Property. The book you just read is protected by Instant IP<sup>IP</sup>, a proprietary process, which integrates blockchain technology giving Intellectual Property "Global Protection." By creating a "Time-Stamped" smart contract that can never be tampered with or changed, we establish "First Use" that tracks back to the author.

Instant IP<sup>IP</sup> functions much like a Pre-Patent since it provides an immutable "First Use" of the Intellectual Property. This is achieved through our proprietary process of leveraging blockchain technology and smart contracts. As a result, proving "First Use" is simple through a global and verifiable smart contract. By protecting intellectual property with blockchain technology and smart contracts, we establish a "First to File" event.

Protected by Instant IP<sup>IP</sup>

# LEARN MORE AT INSTANTIP.TODAY